C000229360

What readers are saying about A

A Different Dream for My Child offers the
everything seems wrong. The author's pe...
ers; her prayers express what grieving pa...
tive postscripts nudge readers to move past ...
book is like a gentle balm prescribed for persons bruised and battered by circumstances.

Holly G. Miller
The Saturday Evening Post

Powerful, insightful, and candidly honest, Jolene Philo's book *A Different Dream for My Child* is a treasured companion for those who've journeyed the heart-bending path of caring for a chronically or critically ill child. Written with insight, passion, and wisdom, Jolene's words deliver both comfort and biblical counsel on the diverse and complex emotional, spiritual, relational, and practical aspects of caring for sick children. This book is a celebration of hope in the God of comfort who walks beside us in the midst of our pain.

Shelly Beach
Award-winning author of *Precious Lord, Take My Hand*
and *Ambushed by Grace*

The trauma and drama of a sick child is a journey of its own kind. Gratefully Jolene has tenderly come to the heart-aid of these families. If you have experienced or are living in deep sorrow brought on by your child's condition I recommend that you open this book and allow the balm of understanding to meet you where you are at . . . to help ease your ongoing ache, your loneliness, and your feelings of isolation.

Patsy Clairmont
Author of *Catching Fireflies* and Women of Faith® Speaker

No words can change the diagnosis, but there are those who can help parents change their attitude. Jolene Philo understands those cries because of the experience with her son, Allen. I highly recommend this book from a mother who opens her heart on every page.

Cecil Murphey
New York Times best-selling author of more than 100 books,
including *When Someone You Love Has Cancer*

What a tremendously helpful and inspiring book! Having two chronically ill children myself, I was amazed at how well acquainted Philo was with the private pain, grief, guilt, and loneliness I have experienced trying to cope with it all. With each devotion, my spirit was lifted into a hope I have rarely felt in the midst of the battle. I highly recommend this book to any parent whose dreams for their children have been sidetracked by illness.

Rene Gutteridge
Author of *Never the Bride* and *My Life as a Doormat*

The examples of comfort and shared experience will benefit all who read this book. Chronic sorrow follows chronic disease, and the reflections offered are excellent in addressing this. Every problem discussed is "right on" and pulls out personal recollections of many of my patients. I would recommend it to families and caretakers alike.

David H. Van Dyke MD
Pediatric Neurologist

A Different dream for My Child

Meditations for Parents of Critically and Chronically Ill Children

DISCOVERY HOUSE

PUBLISHERS®

Discovery House Publishers is affiliated with RBC Ministries, Grand Rapids, Michigan.

Discovery House books are distributed to the trade exclusively by Barbour Publishing, Inc., Uhrichsville, Ohio.

Requests for permission to quote from this book should be directed to: Permissions Department, Discovery House Publishers, P.O. Box 3566, Grand Rapids, MI 49501.

Scripture quotations are from *THE MESSAGE*. Copyright © by Eugene H. Peterson 1993, 1994, 1995, 1996, 2000, 2001, 2002. Used by permission of NavPress Publishing Group. Also, as noted, from *The New American Standard Bible*, © Copyright 1960, 1962, 1963, 1968, 1971, 1972, 1973, 1975, 1977, 1995 by The Lockman Foundation. Used by permission.

Interior design by Melissa Elenbaas

Library of Congress Cataloging-in-Publication Data

Philo, Jolene.
   A different dream for my child : meditations for parents of critically and chronically ill children / Jolene Philo.
       p. cm.
   ISBN 978-1-57293-307-1
   1. Parents—Prayers and devotions. 2. Chronically ill children.
3. Critically ill children. I. Title.
   BV4845.P45 2009
   242' .4—dc22

Printed in the United States of America

09 10 11 12 13 /   / 10 9 8 7 6 5 4 3 2 1

Contents

Section Three
Conflicting Dreams—Juggling Two Worlds

Section Six
A Different Dream Begins—Raising a Survivor

Introduction

My husband, Hiram, and I had been married four years when we learned our first child was on the way. The doctor said the baby would come in late May of 1982, which fit perfectly into my schoolteacher's schedule. I would have a whole summer to spend with our baby before I went back to work.

The day after the school year ended, I went into labor late in the evening. We hopped into the car and raced to the hospital. Our son, Allen Craig Philo, was born shortly after midnight on Sunday, May 23. Efficiency nut that I am, I was a bit smug about the timing. Not one day of summer had been lost to an overdue birth. Labor and delivery had been easy. Our baby was cute as a button. Life was good, and my dream summer as a first-time mom was about to begin.

By morning, my dream had turned into a nightmare. Doctors discovered that our son, so perfect on the outside, had a life-threatening birth defect, and Allen was flown to a hospital 700 miles away for immediate surgery. We caught up with him two days later.

Instead of spending the summer at home with a new baby, we spent much of it in a hospital in an unfamiliar city. When we finally brought our baby home, complications slowed his recovery. During the first five years of his life, Allen was hospitalized several more times, and we were at his side through it all.

Our son remembers very little about what happened. My husband and I remember it vividly. We were grateful to be with our son. But we were so far from home, without friends and family to comfort us, and the hospital offered little support to displaced parents. We felt utterly and completely alone.

Over the years support networks for parents have improved, but most only provide for immediate basic needs. Not enough guidance is provided for parents like you, devastated and confused by your own broken dreams, full of questions about why God would allow pain and suffering in the life of an innocent child.

The devotions in this book were written to address your spiritual needs. As I interviewed families, I saw you standing by a small hospital bed, sitting in a surgery waiting room, speaking to a doctor. And I have prayed that the stories of these families, who have been where you are now, can bring you hope in the midst of lost dreams.

The parents chronicled in this book had great dreams for their children. When their children became ill and their dreams changed, they slowly, and sometimes painfully, embraced the different dream God had fashioned for their children and found joy.

They want you to discover joy in your new dream, too. They are cheering for you as you persevere. They are praying for you as you embrace God's dream for your family. May their wisdom and faith encourage and assure you of the truth they have learned through their children's struggles: God is with your child, and He is with you, too.

You are not alone.

> God is striding ahead of you. He's right there
> with you. He won't let you down; he won't
> leave you. Don't be intimidated. Don't worry.
>
> Deuteronomy 31:8

To my husband, Hiram, who walked every step of our different dream with me.

And to our children, Allen and Anne, who are my dreams come true.

Section

1

A Different Dream Begins

Diagnosis

Something's Wrong with Your Child

The Lord is near to the brokenhearted
And saves those who are crushed in spirit.
Psalm 34:18 (NASB)

Do you want a girl or a boy?"

I heard that question often when we were expecting our first child. My pat answer was, "I don't care, so long as the baby is healthy."

I was convinced God would honor my selfless desire since my husband, Hiram, and I were model parents-to-be. We'd planned for this child. We attended every prenatal appointment and practiced Lamaze. I ate right, exercised, and dreamed about the birth of our perfect new baby.

The first clue that my dream was not God's plan came the morning after our son, Allen, was born, when the doctor sat down in a chair near the foot of my bed. (Over the next few years, I learned it's not a good sign when a doctor sits beside a hospital bed.)

"Something's wrong," he told me, and with those words, my dreams evaporated. Love for the child who had grown inside me pressed heavy against my heart until it broke. Fear of what lay ahead crushed my spirit.

When the doctor told you something was wrong with your child, your life changed, too. The world you dreamed about before your baby's birth—of diapers and breast feeding, sleep deprivation and exhausted joy—turned into a nightmare of Life Flight transport and neonatal intensive care.

Or perhaps the days you once spent chasing a healthy toddler were replaced with hours beside a hospital bed holding a still, small hand.

Or your busy soccer mom afternoons spent driving from school to lessons to practice became a dizzying blur of technicians and lab tests and painful procedures.

This new world of hospitals and doctors and medical abnormalities breaks your heart and crushes your spirit. You can't bear to see your child because the hurt on that small face pierces your heart. But you can't stay away because you want to comfort your child. So you stumble along, desperate for a God who will strengthen you so you can support your child. But you wonder if the God who allowed your child's suffering cares enough to meet your needs.

Those thoughts shook my faith the day the doctor sat beside my bed. *Would a loving God allow this? Does He care about our child? Are you there, God?* I wondered.

Then my husband arrived, heard the news, and sensed my despair. He asked a few questions before the doctor left. When we were alone, he said, "Jolene, let's pray." I nodded, and he took my hand. "Thank you, Father, for giving Allen to us. He's yours, God, not ours. You loved him before we knew him, and he belongs to you. Be with him when we can't. Amen."

Hiram has always been a man of few words. He struggles to speak his thoughts and often doesn't try, knowing that I have enough words to fill any silence. But on a day when my heart was broken, my spirit crushed, and my faith gone, God gave Hiram strength to speak the words I couldn't say. And clinging to my husband's hand, in deep silence and through many tears, I sensed that God was very near.

Dear God, my heart is breaking for my child today. My spirit is crushed by fear of what lies ahead. I can't find words to pray, Father, so please pray for me. Be near to my child and be near to me today as your word promises.

How has God used people to strengthen you when your spirit was crushed? How can the Bible help you pray when you can't find words? Who could you ask to pray for you when you can't?

Take Time to Reflect

2

The Blackest Black

Then I said to myself, "Oh, he even sees me in
the dark!
At night I'm immersed in the light!"
It's a fact: darkness isn't dark to you;
night and day, darkness and light, they're
all the same to you.

Psalm 139:11–12

Our son's diagnosis came within a day of his birth, and it changed our world. For other parents, the diagnosis and the life changes that accompany it come when a child is still in the womb. Sandy was four months pregnant when she experienced bleeding and went in for an ultrasound. The doctor ran some tests and said the bleeding would correct itself. "But there's another problem," he told Sandy and her husband, Wayne. "Your son is anencephalic. He doesn't have a brain."

With those words, Sandy's world went dark. "It was the blackest black I can ever describe," she said, "like being in a cave when they shut the lights out. You feel like you're going to suffocate."

Wayne remembers the day, too. "I was devastated. We had no idea that anything was wrong. Then you get this news. And it just yanks your heart out."

You know how Wayne and Sandy felt. You have experienced the darkness, the sense of suffocation, the devastation of an unexpected diagnosis that has life-changing implications for your child and your family. When the news comes, things look so black you don't think you will ever see light again. You don't want to tell others because you don't want their light extinguished, too. And you can't bring yourself to pray because if God is light, like He says He is, why is He allowing such darkness to surround your precious child?

Your thoughts are a normal reaction to the news you've received. They are part of the grief process, no matter your child's age or prognosis, as you grieve the loss of a normal, healthy life for your child. But you can't sit alone grieving in the dark. People want to help you find your way through it. So pick up the phone and share the bad news with those who love you. Reach out to your spouse and describe how you feel. Ask God, who says He is light, your hard questions. Because when you cry out from your darkness, light will slowly return.

In small, unexpected ways God brought light back into our world. When we told our family and friends, they cried with us and prayed with us, and a little light seeped in. I called the financial officer at work about our health insurance, and her reassurance about our coverage brought more light. Every nurse or CNA (Certified Nursing Assistant) in the hospital brought a bag of sample products to my room, and this growing pile of kindness touched my heart and brightened my darkness. God listened to my hard questions over the next days and months and years. Slowly He answered them until, finally, the gloom lifted completely and our world was light again.

Sandy described how God used Wayne to dispel some of her darkness. "In that hospital room that day, Wayne did something that I'll never forget. I can shut my eyes and see him standing there in front of that window, praying. Immediately, that blackness left and God's presence was there. The feeling still makes my hair stand on end when I talk about it because I know God came in that room. And His presence was there. It didn't make it okay, but we just knew that God was with us."

He's with you, too, right now. He'll reveal himself in your circumstances, and He'll use people to do it. So reach out and let Him lead you to His light.

Dear God, blackness surrounds me and my child today. I can't imagine ever seeing light again. Help me find my way through this darkness. Bring someone to show me the way back to your light.

Who do you know who will cry with you, understand you, and love you as you ask God hard questions? Who can bring God's light to your darkness?

Take Time to Reflect

3

Snap Decisions

If you don't know what you're doing, pray to
the Father. He loves to help.
You'll get his help, and won't be condescended
to when you ask for it.
Ask boldly, believingly, without a second
thought.

James 1:5

Snap decisions are not my forte, even under the best of circumstances. When I have to make them in stressful situations, I'm pathetic. So I often wonder how I, under the worst imaginable conditions, managed to make the snap decision that determined my son's medical treatment.

I was twenty-five years old and weak from loss of blood during my son's delivery eight hours earlier. The hospital was ninety miles from the remote town where we lived, and our closest relative was a day's drive away. Hiram was at the home of an acquaintance, taking a shower. I was lying in my hospital bed waiting for him to return, wondering what was happening to our newborn son.

The room didn't have a phone, and cell phones were still the stuff of science fiction. So when the call came from the Rapid City hospital, where our son had been transferred, someone wheeled me to the nurses' station to talk to the doctor.

When I picked up the phone, a pediatrician I'd never seen blindsided me with news I didn't want to hear. "Mrs. Philo, your son has a tracheal-esophageal fistula. His esophagus comes down from his throat and forms a blind pouch. It comes up from his stomach and hooks into his trachea. The corrective surgery has a success rate of over 90 percent, but he needs to be flown to Denver or Omaha immediately. Where do you want him to go?"

The diagnosis was more than my mind could absorb. I couldn't think. "My husband will be here soon. Can we talk it over and call you back?"

The doctor's voice was compassionate but also insistent. "The sooner your baby has surgery, the fewer complications there will be."

I felt completely alone, though a half dozen nurses and med techs clustered around the desk, eavesdropping on the conversation. I wanted to cry. I wanted to hide. But my baby's tiny face and the solid weight of him, which I had felt only twice before the ambulance whisked him away, wouldn't let me do either. Somehow my mind cleared. I remembered that, in a life far removed from this present nightmare, my parents lived in a small Iowa town a few hours from Omaha. And I knew that to weather this storm, Hiram and I needed family around us.

"Omaha," I said, and the nurses let out a collective sigh. "Send him to Omaha." Then I hung up the phone and began to cry.

You have probably been confronted with snap decisions, also. And no matter how many counselors advised you, in the end you alone had to make the decision that determined the course of your child's life—because you're the parent, and you love your child.

More decisions may lie ahead for you. You'll feel too young, too inexperienced, and too ignorant for the task. Still, you'll decide to the best of your ability. And you won't be alone as you decide. Whether you feel God's presence or not, the Father who dearly loves you will clear your mind and guide every decision made with a heart of love for your child.

I know it will happen to you. Because when it happened to me, somehow I knew the right answer—Omaha.

Dear Father, my mind is confused, and I'm so afraid I'll make wrong decisions for my child. Clear my mind and guide me. Give me your wisdom and confidence so I can decide well.

How have you sensed God guiding you as you make decisions for your child? How has He honored those decisions? Who can give you wise counsel and comfort as you make more decisions?

Take Time to Reflect

4

Call in the Forces

For day by day men came to David to help him,
until there was a great army like the army of
God.

1 Chronicles 12:22 (NASB)

If you're a parent who just received a difficult diagnosis concerning your child, listen to Carolyn's words. "If you can know the diagnosis is the absolute worst," she says, "that can help."

She knows what she's talking about. In May of 1981, her ten-month-old daughter Beth had a sore arm and was fussy. Since Beth had suffered a bout of spinal meningitis in February, Carolyn took her to the doctor. And since Carolyn suspected she was pregnant again, she took a urine sample in, too.

Carolyn was right on both counts. She was pregnant. And her concern about Beth was justified. The doctor suspected leukemia and referred them to a nearby regional hospital for more tests. There, Carolyn and her husband, Jeff, were told that lab tests confirmed their doctor's suspicions. Beth had leukemia.

Immediately mother and daughter were whisked by ambulance to a university hospital for treatment. Jeff followed in their car. But once they arrived, they waited a long time until the type of leukemia was determined. "It was a weekend," Carolyn explained. "Labs were shut down and people were on vacation. It seemed like we waited for days. And then it was not good news. They said it was the type of leukemia forty-year-old men get. At that point in time, survival rate for that type was one out of four."

Nothing, Carolyn said, compared to receiving the diagnosis. "It was the worst. Nothing compares to that. In my mind, dying is nothing compared to the diagnosis."

Parents who have experienced a dreaded diagnosis recognize the truth in her words. Before the diagnosis, parents have a thousand sick kid scenarios bouncing through their brains. *It could be this. Or it could be that. Or this. Or that.* The diseases and their possible manifestations march by in an unceasing parade that holds them in the grip of paralyzing fear.

When the diagnosis is made, all those anxieties funnel into the one disease or condition or syndrome afflicting their child. And that moment, when the enemy is identified but not yet understood, when parents grapple with the diagnosis and stare it in the face, is as big and frightening as it is ever going to be.

So if you are all alone, wrestling with a diagnosis and its implications for your child's life, take heart. This is the absolute worst moment. That means it's going to get better, and Carolyn knows why. "Because after that, you call in the forces. You call in the doctors, you pray, you have people praying for you. You get a plan. You live again."

So prepare to live again. Call in the forces. God has an army of doctors and nurses and medical personnel ready to battle your child's physical enemies. And He has a whole army of loved ones and friends and chaplains and counselors ready to pray down the spiritual enemies attacking your family. So call in the forces and watch God muster soldiers to support you.

Don't discount anyone God musters into your army. One of the most powerful soldiers in Jeff and Carolyn's army was their unborn son, Justin. "Being pregnant forced me to take care of myself. It gave me a reason to take care of myself," Carolyn says. "Justin was a gift of grace."

It's time for you to do what Jeff and Carolyn did. Call in your forces and trust God to form your army. And then, take heart. It's time to live again.

Dear God, our child's diagnosis has laid us low. We face so many uncertainties. We don't know what treatment will be like or if it will be effective. We don't know what kind of life our child will have. So send reinforcements to lift us up and give us hope.

What has been your lowest point since your child became sick? Who did God send to be part of your army? What forces do you still need to call in?

Take Time to Reflect

5

Don't Drive Alone

A friend loves at all times,
And a brother is born for adversity.
Proverbs 17:17 (NASB)

Most people in their right minds would agree that a father who has just heard his child's serious, perhaps life-threatening diagnosis should not be driving a car. But fathers who have just received such a diagnosis are not in their right minds. The only thing on their minds is to take action; and the only thing they can think of to do is get to the hospital as quickly as possible.

That's what one father, Lyn, did in 1964 when he got a call at the school where he worked. His wife, Sherri, was seven and a half months pregnant when she told a friend she was having back pain. The friend took Sherri to her doctor thirty miles away. An X-ray showed the baby had no brain.

Sherri says, "The nurse called the school to tell Lyn he should come, but that there was nothing life-threatening, because he didn't want Lyn in an accident. But you know he's going to get alarmed, just wondering, Why did they call me to come?"

Lyn agrees with Sherri. "You know something's not normal. You don't have to be a mental giant to figure that one out." Fortunately, even though Lyn drove alone, he made it to the hospital without an accident.

But Lyn, and every other father I have talked to who has driven alone in similar circumstances, has the same advice: don't drive alone. Get someone to go with you, even if making the arrangements slows you down. Because the one thing you can do right now, the one thing God calls you to do is to be with your wife and child in a hospital room.

You'll feel helpless sitting there. You'll deceive yourself and think you aren't doing anything. But think about how devastated your family would be if you weren't there because you had an accident on the way to be with them, and the right thing to do will be obvious. Right now being with your family is everything, and asking someone to drive you there is essential. So do it.

Years ago, Jeff drove across the state alone, following the ambulance carrying his wife, Carolyn, and daughter Beth, after she was diagnosed with leukemia. Later, he took a lot of flak from his friends for not asking them to drive with him. Jeff admits that he blindly followed that ambulance, his mind with his daughter and his wife, not on his driving. "You should have called," his friends said, "and we would have driven you over there."

At the time, the diagnosis blew Jeff away. He couldn't think straight enough to ask someone to take him. But Jeff and Lyn and other fathers who have been where you are today don't want you to do what they did. God is giving you their stories so you can think clearly and choose intelligently, so you will be safe and whole and present with your struggling family.

So ask a friend or a brother to drive. If you're stranded far away from family and friends, ask people at the hospital to help you find a driver. Ask the doctors, ask the nurses, ask the hospital chaplain. Keep asking until you get what you need. Refuse to take no for an answer.

Remember, you have a family, and your family needs you more than they need heroic strength and blind action. Your presence in that hospital room is God's best for all of you. They need you and you need them.

So please, don't drive alone.

Dear Father, I feel so helpless and inadequate. I can't even drive alone to the hospital where my sick child is waiting. Help me lay down my pride and ask for assistance. Please bring a friend or a brother to get me to my family safely so I can be where I need to be.

When is it hard for you to admit that if you get behind the wheel you'll be driving blind? What will convince you to make a safe choice and ask for help? Who do you know who will drive you if you ask?

Take Time to Reflect

6

What Did I Do Wrong?

Have I sinned? What have I done to You,
O watcher of men?

Job 7:20 (NASB)

Before the fallout from our son's diagnosis had time to settle, before any urgent calls could be made, before my son was flown away for surgery, the questions began. *What did I do to cause this? Was it the two drinks I had at the wedding rehearsal before I knew I was pregnant? Or is it a punishment from God for something from my past?*

I'm not the only mom who has engaged in self-inflicted torture. When Brenda learned that both her son and daughter had crippling arthrogryposis, a condition that weakens joints and muscles, similar questions plagued her. "I had lots of internal conversations. 'I must have caused this,' or

'Something I did caused it.' You just go through that. Maybe not everybody else does, but I did."

Angie agrees. Her son Chandler completed three years of successful cancer treatment the year he turned ten. "Even now, it drives me nuts. Did I drink something when I was pregnant? Did I breathe in something and the fumes were too much? Did I get bad chicken? That is a big monster to wrestle with."

Dads torture themselves, too. Chuck thought he was responsible for his children's medical conditions. His first son was born with both liver and bowel outside of his body. His second son died at birth because a bronchogenic cyst blocked his airway. "I always thought it was my fault. I thought maybe my partying at college had ruined my gene pool. I felt responsible. I felt a lot of guilt."

Self-blame also tortured Lyn when his daughter was born without a brain. Since his nephew had been born severely mentally retarded, his mind made a predictable jump to his own child's condition. "I was the dad," said Lyn. "It was my fault."

Many parents of sick children wrestle with the guilt monster. But if it pins you down, it can paralyze you. So quit torturing yourself with unanswerable questions and useless blame. To stop the thoughts, tell someone else what you're thinking. That's what I did, and when I confided in Hiram, his face became grave. "Those are lies, Jolene," he said. "Don't listen to them. You're a good mother."

My husband was right. The self-inflicted blame and the questions were lies. They were whispers from an enemy who wanted to turn my thoughts to inward torture rather than to the God of comfort. My enemy wanted me to focus on a past I couldn't alter instead of on the present where God had work for me to do. Even if the doctors had found a correlation between my behavior and my child's condition, God wouldn't have wanted me to wallow in guilt. He would want me to admit my mistake and seek His strength to change the way I live.

That's why you need to voice your guilty questions, too. The minute you do and someone speaks truth back to you, the lies in your head will be mortally wounded. They'll try to resurrect themselves now and then, but truth is too strong for them and they will slowly bleed away.

Your child doesn't need a parent paralyzed by guilt. Your child needs a parent empowered and motivated by the truth. So give voice to the unrelenting whispers in your head and wait for God to speak eternal, comforting truth that will change your heart.

Dear God of truth, please stop the whispers in my head. Please expose the lies that lead to guilt and isolation and shame. Speak truth and open my ears so I can hear it. Lead me to your truth so I am present for my child.

What guilty questions have plagued you since your child's diagnosis? What questions can you ask the doctor or chaplain to dispel your guilt?

Take Time to Reflect

7

Second Opinions

Refuse good advice and watch your plans fail;
take good counsel and watch them succeed.
Proverbs 15:22

Right now, if you've had some time to adjust to your child's diagnosis, you're ready to sort through the avalanche of medical information you've been given. As you move beyond reactionary shock to reasonable thought, you'll start asking questions about prognosis and treatment options and doctor qualifications. And you may wonder if asking for a second opinion is something you should do.

Jenny, a young woman of twenty-six and a survivor of acute lymphocytic leukemia (ALL), has this to say about the issue. "My advice is to be sure to get second opinions.

Go to a medical center that is updated and has advanced technology. A second opinion confirms the diagnosis and allows you to move forward instead of not knowing or second-guessing things."

Jenny has good reason to say this. Her ALL diagnosis came when she was four years old. When tests showed she had a highly treatable form of leukemia, her mom and dad, living in a small North Dakota community, took Jenny to a university hospital in another state for a second opinion. The doctor at the university hospital, who was very experienced and had compiled a high patient survival rate, was impressed with the referring doctor's astute and speedy diagnosis. Knowing Jenny had been in good hands since the very beginning made it easier for her parents to move forward and make decisions.

Asking for a second opinion doesn't indicate a lack of faith in God's provision for your child. Instead, it shows a willingness to follow His advice to seek the counsel of wise people and to make use of the resources He provides.

Your doctor should encourage you to get a second opinion. One pediatrician says, "I think the family, especially a young parent, should feel comfortable asking questions of their provider. You need to feel comfortable with your second opinion, and if you don't, you should feel comfortable seeking another."

But she adds a caution. "If you ask those questions again and you get a similar answer or a similar diagnosis, at some point you have to feel, as a parent, that you've asked all the questions. Then you have to settle."

If you want a second opinion, get one. If the opinions agree, move forward. If they don't, get another one, and continue until you believe that you have explored every reasonable possibility for your child and found the best possible treatment. If your doctor makes you feel uncomfortable when you ask questions, ask anyway. Be insistent, for your child's sake.

But realize that at some point, once you've gathered all the opinions and are sure of the diagnosis, you must make a decision on behalf of your child. Remember, the purpose of obtaining a second opinion is to allow you to move forward with confidence rather than wallow in indecision.

Make your decision based on the opinions you have gathered, and then rest in the assurance that you have been the best possible advocate for your child. Know that God has heard your prayers for wisdom and a clear head.

Move forward, confident that He knows how much you love your child and is pleased with what you have done on your little one's behalf.

Dear Father, the medical experts and their information are intimidating. I have to make decisions about things I didn't even know existed until recently. Lead me to people and resources I need to be a wise advocate for my precious child.

Where can you go to learn more about your child's diagnosis and treatment? What kind of information will assist your decision-making? What questions should you ask the doctor when you see him next?

Take Time to Reflect

8

Your Dreams Change

"I prayed for this child, and God gave me what
I asked for. And now I have dedicated him
to God. He's dedicated to God for life."

1 Samuel 1:27–28

A diagnosis can come suddenly, a quick and unexpected shock. Or it can come slowly, after numerous visits to the doctor, long after you first suspect your child is battling something seriously wrong. But however it happens, one thing is the same for parents of really sick kids: their dreams change.

Doug and Brenda's dreams have changed often since their children were born. When Jeff was born in 1982, they didn't know he had any medical issues. But he was very weak and spent a month in the hospital. Doug says that at that point, "We didn't like it and didn't know why it happened. But I thought, okay, I can probably get through this."

As time went on, physical therapy didn't resolve Jeff's physical issues, and he was diagnosed with arthrogryposis, a genetic disorder that affects joints and muscles. Brenda says that's when their expectations for Jeff began to change. "I can remember we'd always say, 'Well, okay, Jeff can't be a football player,' when we found out the physical aspect. 'But, he'll be a doctor.'"

Their perspective shifted again several years later when Jeff's mental retardation, a condition completely separate from the arthrogryposis, was confirmed. Doug said accepting the second diagnosis was difficult. "The physical limitations you could work around. The mental limitations were much more serious."

A year and a half after Jeff was born, before his retardation was evident, Doug and Brenda decided to add to their family. Doctors said they had a one in four chance of having another child with a similar physical condition. So Brenda prayed, "Please, God, don't let me get pregnant if anything's going to happen." When she discovered she was expecting, she thought God had honored her prayer. After all, the baby in her womb was more active than Jeff had been a few years earlier.

Brenda describes her daughter's birth in 1984. "I could see Doug when Jessica was born. I remember the look on his face. She was affected, too. But I didn't know how much." Once more their dreams changed, even though their little girl's physical limitations were less severe than Jeff's and her mental abilities were not affected at all.

According to Doug, it's not always easy to embrace the new reality that accompanies a diagnosis. "I wasn't able to experience a lot of things you normally expect to experience with a son. It's somewhat the same with Jessica. At times, I almost feel like I've missed out on something. But from the other side of it, we've had experiences nobody else in the world will ever know unless they have a special needs child. So there are trade-offs."

Trade-offs and changes in perspective will accompany your child's diagnosis, too. Over the coming days and weeks, and perhaps for the rest of your child's life, you'll discover them. Accepting these changes will take time and prayer. You'll wonder if God knows what He's doing, and you'll wonder if you can trust Him.

If you decide to trust Him and cling to Him through this crisis, His plans for your child will slowly become your new dreams. That's what happened to Brenda. "I pray for whatever level Jeff's at, because of the mental retardation, that he will know Jesus at whatever level that is. I have to believe that God knows and God will answer that prayer."

Brenda's ultimate dream for her children is the same dream other parents have for their children, whether or not they have special needs. We dream of being in heaven together one day with our children, whole and completely healed, praising the God who gave us and our children the gift of life.

Father of all dreams, I'm struggling to lay down my old dreams for my child and embrace new ones. Show me how to accept what is, instead of clinging to what might have been. Give me new hope for my child, and teach me to rejoice in it.

What dreams did you have for your child before this diagnosis? Which dreams are hardest to release? What new dreams do you have that will bring joy to you and your child in these hard circumstances?

Take Time to Reflect

9

Aching Arms

But our God turned the curse into a blessing.

Nehemiah 13:2

A mother's arms are made to hold children. The shape is right—the crook in the arm creating a circle from shoulder to elbow to wrist to chest. And the size is right—a newborn fits exactly within it, a toddler's torso snuggles perfectly into the same space, and a youngster's expanding shoulders fill it completely.

Every mother unable to hold her hurting child because of medical treatment has endured the agony of empty, aching arms. I first felt it during our two-day drive across South Dakota and Nebraska, on the way to the Omaha hospital where our son was recovering from surgery. I told my husband that my arms hurt. He thought I meant my muscles ached.

"No, my arms ache to hold Allen," I explained. "It feels like a curse." Hiram gave me a long, slow look and drove a little faster.

I thought the ache would recede when I held my son again. But I was wrong. Wires and tubes kept me from holding him close enough. Constant procedures and monitor checks and doctor examinations kept me from holding him long enough. Throughout the sleepless nights in our rented room, the ache never left me during the endless, dark hours that Allen was outside of my embrace.

As he healed from surgery, the number of tubes and wires attached to him dwindled. One day—one great day—he was tube-free. He looked like a normal baby, as long as his sleeper hid the scars crisscrossing his stomach and back. The nurse smiled and handed him, wrapped tightly in a blanket, to me. I sat in a rocking chair and held my baby in the circle of my arms.

All around us, ventilators breathed air into infant lungs, monitors beeped incessantly, nurses cared for tiny patients, and the thin cries of premature babies filled the room. I heard none of it, saw none of it. All of me was concentrated on the bundle in my arms.

We rocked for a long time, back and forth, back and forth. As we rocked, my ache melted away and was replaced by an unexpected gratitude. As we rocked, I grew thankful for the days when I ached to hold my baby, for the nights when the ache kept me awake. For had my arms never ached, I could not have cherished enough this intimate moment with my son. Had my arms never ached, I couldn't have understood the privilege of holding a hungry, healthy child to my breast in the dark hours of the night. Had my arms never ached, I could never have whispered, "Thank you," as God turned the curse of my silent, empty arms to blessed fullness of joy.

If your arms are aching today, if the ache is consuming you, the last thing you want to do is thank God for the pain. But you are standing at a crossroads where you need to make a choice, an unwanted choice, a difficult choice. Either trust God to bring a blessing out of this curse, or turn away from Him because you don't believe He will.

The moment you trust Him to change your curse into blessing, a transformation will begin. God will open your eyes to the blessings around you, blessings you would not have recognized without the curse of your child's diagnosis. His arms will envelop you, and, safe in His embrace, a host of blessings other parents never see will become your joy.

When that happens, you will be overcome with gratitude. As this curse becomes a blessing, you may even surprise yourself and whisper, "Thank you, Father, for aching arms."

God, my arms ache today. I long to hold my child close, but I can't. Why have you allowed this curse into our lives? Give me faith beyond what I possess so I will trust you to turn this curse into a blessing. Give me new eyes to see the blessings you provide.

When do your arms ache to hold your child? What do you regard as curses in your life today? What needs to happen so you will trust God to turn them into blessings during this hard time?

Take Time to Reflect

Stuck in a Bad Dream

Hospital Life

10

Scrubbing In

> Let us draw near with a sincere heart in full assurance of faith, having our hearts sprinkled clean from an evil conscience and our bodies washed with pure water.
>
> Hebrews 10:22 (NASB)

Our son was born on a Sunday, shortly after midnight. Before midnight came again, he'd had his first airplane ride, undergone major surgery, and was recovering in a neonatal intensive care unit (NICU) 700 miles away from the hospital where he was born. Nearly two days later, yearning to see Allen, my husband and I, along with my mother and a cousin, arrived at the NICU where our baby was a patient.

Allen's primary care nurse greeted us. "Before you see him, you need to scrub in and put on gowns." We all nodded and smiled, but my heart sank. I was desperate to see my baby. This silly hospital protocol was another delay that was keeping me from bonding with our son.

We put on paper caps and gowns. Then we stood over the stainless steel basin and scrubbed our hands with harsh antiseptic soap. "Scrub for five minutes," the sign above the sink instructed. I dutifully lathered my hands and arms, but inwardly I fumed. *I want to see my baby. My baby needs to see me. Why do I have to do this?* Precious seconds of my son's life washed away while soapy water swirled down the drain.

I stood at that sink and scrubbed, and my tears dropped hard and fast. They splashed onto my scrub brush and ran down my arm. As they fell, a new picture challenged my self-pity. I saw the germs on my hands being washed away, far from where they could weaken my helpless child. As the water gurgled down the drain, my thoughts no longer swirled around my emotions. Instead, I considered what was best for our baby. He needed parents washed clean of every speck of contamination that could compromise his health. He needed parents whose presence would strengthen rather than weaken him.

In that moment, my attitude changed. I appreciated the hospital's efforts to protect our son from the germs on my skin. And suddenly, I also realized that my own inner being needed as much cleansing as my outer one, but no water the hospital provided could penetrate the deep recesses of my heart. So I asked the One who waters my soul to cleanse me. "God, forgive me for putting my needs ahead of my son's. Wash me clean of such thoughts, and teach me to be the mother he needs."

The scrub sink protocol of 1982 is long gone, replaced by other practices research has proven are more effective in protecting sick children. Some of the new rules and procedures may seem pointless to you. They may even seem detrimental or cruel or painful. You may perceive them as a wall, an obstruction in your relationship with your child. You may be angry about the procedures, like I was, and think of the hospital as an enemy instead of as an ally.

When those thoughts invade your heart, examine your inner being. Are you carrying the germs of a self-pitying, victim mentality that could hurt your child's mind much as any virus or bacteria can hurt the body? If so, ask the One who shed His blood to give you new life, to sprinkle your heart clean of anything that might cause you to hinder your child's inward recovery. Ask Him to strengthen you so you can anticipate and meet your child's physical, emotional, and spiritual needs.

As long as you're in this hospital world, whenever you need His water, ask and ask and ask again. Let His love wash over you until you are ready to return to your child with a clean and quiet heart.

Dear Father, this hospital world is strange to me, and everything that has happened is affecting my emotions and my attitude. Reveal and wash away any wrong emotions and wrong attitudes within me that could infect and weaken my child.

What hospital protocols and procedures don't you agree with or understand? Who can you consult to find out their purpose? How can you phrase your questions so they are concerned rather than combative?

Take Time to Reflect

11

Words of Peace

> People with their minds set on you,
> you keep completely whole.
>
> Isaiah 26:3

Hospital life can make you crazy, especially when your child's health is tenuous. It's hard to stay calm in an environment where your child is continually poked and prodded, where your normal, daily routine is totally disrupted, where you face the reality of loss and grief. But this is the world you and your child inhabit, at least for a while.

The bad news is that you have to find peace in this strange place or you will go crazy and be of no use to your child. The good news is that God was at the hospital long before you, making preparations to help you find peace.

Sandy knows God was at work long before she and Wayne received the diagnosis that their unborn baby had no brain, months before her hospital stay after Baby Ethan was born. "It was a day or two before Ethan's diagnosis. I don't know what we were studying. I can't remember what the situation was, but I have the date written in my Bible by Isaiah 26:3. That was in April." The scripture God gave Sandy before the diagnosis carried her through the dark days after they got the news. It comforted her during the sleepless nights of her pregnancy as she carried to full term a baby who would die at birth.

After Sandy delivered Ethan in August, she stayed in the emergency room for a while. "Then they put me in a labor and delivery room. Then in a regular patient's recovery room." On the wall in that room was a poster with the words of Isaiah 26:3 written on it: "He will keep thee in perfect peace whose mind is stayed upon Me."

The memory of that event makes Sandy shake her head. "What are the odds of that Scripture being on a poster on the wall?" The words assured Sandy of God's active presence in her circumstances before Ethan was born. And that knowledge was the source of great peace during and long after her hospital stay. "God kept reminding me of that Scripture. And it would always bring me peace. It would always settle me down and calm me in my spirit."

God was present during our son's hospitalization, too, though He didn't reveal himself through a poster on the wall. Instead He spoke His comfort and peace through the mouths of strangers. An ordinary hospital accounts manager looked at our health insurance policy, shook his head in amazement, and said, "I've never seen such complete coverage before." Allen's primary care nurse in NICU told us over and over how alert and bright our baby was, how bravely he fought, how quickly he recovered—words that calmed our hearts and strengthened us. And then there were words from family and friends on the phone, visits after supper with people who opened their homes to us, that convinced us God had gone before us to provide peace.

God is present in your circumstances, also. He has prepared words of comfort especially for you, words He knows you need while your child is in the hospital. His words may be written on a poster or in a book. They may be spoken by people around you. They may be a whisper in the depths of your heart. Watch for them, and listen. Set your mind upon God and expect to hear from Him. He's a God who keeps His promises. He will bring you blessed peace.

Dear God of peace, this hospital is driving me crazy, and my mood is affecting my child. I am in need of your calm today. Bring me peace, bring me comfort, and make me whole and strong so I can be the parent my child needs today.

What would help you find peace in your circumstances today? What evidence do you see of God calming your heart? What can you do to share the peace you've experienced with your child and others?

Take Time to Reflect

12

A Gentle Touch

Jesus came over and touched them. "Don't be afraid."

Matthew 17:7

A nurse led us past rows of Isolettes, but we saw only the one where she stopped. Cords dangled from the bank of medical instruments on the wall behind the incubator, but our eyes were fixed upon the tiny form lying in the clear plastic box that was our son's bed.

"Get right next to him," the nurse suggested. Unable to move, we stared at the baby clad only in a diaper. Monitor patches dotted his chest. Wires sprouted from the patches and snaked their way to the machines on the wall. The IV in his arm was splinted in place with a tongue depressor and tape. His torso sprouted two drainage tubes below his ribs and a feeding tube in his stomach. When Susan, the nurse, turned him on his side, we saw the angry, horizontal scar that slashed his upper back from spine to armpit. Nothing could have prepared me for my first look at Allen after his surgery.

Susan smiled and asked, "Would you like to hold him?"

I frowned at the tubes and wires. "How?"

"Not a problem." She moved chairs and rearranged poles, pushed wires and cords away, and motioned for us to sit. She lifted the incubator lid and wrapped Allen in a blanket.

"Will this hurt him?" my husband asked. "We can wait."

"No, he needs to feel your touch." She handed the bundle to Hiram. Allen didn't stir.

While he slept, we did what all parents do. We inspected all ten of his fingers and toes. We marveled at his soft black hair, long upper lip, and wide-set eyes.

Susan teased Hiram. "Are you going to let his mama hold him?" She took Allen and set him in my arms. His lids opened and our eyes locked. He studied my face. Then, I turned until he could see his father. Allen uncurled one fist, and Hiram placed his index finger on that tiny, soft palm. And Allen did what all babies do. He wrapped his small hand tightly around the source of his comfort and love.

A parent's first look at a child of any age, after surgery or a major hospital procedure or an accident, can be pretty grim. Your first reaction to the sight might be to freeze with fear or to back away. But it's vitally important for your child, and for you, to look past the medical paraphernalia and offer the blessing of a loving touch.

Your gentleness speaks safety to your child. Your touch, whether you can wrap your baby in your arms or stroke a toddler's hair or hold a youngster's hand, is the one consistent link between life at home and life in the hospital. Each time you pat your little one and smile into frightened eyes, your touch is a reminder of the comfort and safety of home.

Sometimes while you're at the hospital, you'll be as frightened as your child. When that happens, you need the gentle touch of the loving God who cared enough to send His Son to a world tangled by sickness and disease and pain. Through His Son, God touches our hearts with the promise of life beyond the one we see.

His touch will remind you, as it has reminded frightened people for thousands of years, that true safety and an eternal home exists beyond this tangled world of sickness and disease and pain. Once you wrap your hand around the source of your comfort and love, you can share His blessed comfort with your child.

Dear Father, it's hard to look at my suffering child sometimes. It's hard to touch my little one without passing on my fear and concern. Bless me with a touch from your Son so I can comfort my child.

How did you feel the first time you saw your child in the hospital? What kinds of touch comfort your child? How can you bless your child with your touch?

Take Time to Reflect

13

Be Kind and Gracious

Watch the way you talk ... Say only what helps,
each word a gift.

Ephesians 4:29

During Allen's first hospitalization, my emotions were raw. Hormonal mood swings whacked me every time I turned around. My idea of self-restraint was to let the doctor introduce himself before I launched a volley of questions. The most I could do to control my emotions was to wipe my perpetually tear-stained face and runny nose with tissues instead of my shirtsleeve.

If only I had known Naomi way back then. She's the mother of five children. Two are autistic, one is hyperactive, one has a cleft palette along with major language and speech delays, and one died of a brain tumor as a toddler.

She's spent more time in hospitals than most parents ever will and interacted with more health care professionals than she can count. She knows what it takes to endure long weeks in the hospital with a sick child and repeated hospital stays.

The most important thing to control, she feels, is overly emotional responses when you're under stress. "Always be kind and gracious to the doctors, unless they mess up with your child or something serious. They, next to you, are going to give the child the best care." With that reality in mind, Naomi says sometimes you need to bite your tongue. "'Cause you're emotionally charged anyway, so you may be responding in a way that is inappropriate under normal circumstances."

She issues a caution, too. "Don't change your personality because you're in pain. Don't mistreat people because you're overwhelmed with grief. If you do that, you isolate yourself. And you don't have a support group if you isolate yourself."

But how do you keep from using your circumstances to justify wrong behavior? How do you keep from pushing people away and isolating yourself?

My motivation weighed five pounds, thirteen ounces and was nineteen inches long. I didn't want to teach my newborn to push people away and isolate himself. As he grew, he would watch and listen to everything I did. He was ill and in pain, but he wasn't blind and he wasn't deaf. He would learn how to respond to others through my example.

But I was a basket case; I didn't know where to begin. So God provided someone to mentor me. That someone was my husband, who, even under stress, is a kind and gracious man. When the doctors talked to us after Allen's surgeries, Hiram pondered their words before asking questions. When a nurse came after we turned on Allen's call button, Hiram thanked her before making a request. He thought before speaking and considered alternatives before acting. Thankfully, under his patient tutelage, I started to do the same.

Perhaps you know how to respond with grace and kindness in times of great stress. But if you don't, look for a mentor to teach you. In the end, your gracious words and kind actions will yield two precious gifts. The first, as Naomi mentioned, is immediate: the gift of better care for your child in the hospital. The second gift is your example of how to speak and respond rightly under pressure. That's a gift that will impact your child long after the hospital stay is over, long after the illness and the pain are forgotten, long after your youngster becomes an adult.

Your example has power. Your words have power. So wrap them in kindness and grace. Make your words, even in the hospital, a precious gift to your child.

Dear Father of grace and kindness, how am I supposed to control my words when my child is in the hospital? My emotions push me to say what should remain unsaid, and I can hardly restrain myself. Help me do what is right instead of what is easy. Help me control my words.

When are you most likely to let your pain change your personality? When are you better able to control your responses? How can you train yourself to give your child, and the people caring for your child, the precious gifts produced by kind and gracious words?

Take Time to Reflect

14

Find a Doctor You Can Hug

He put a child in the middle of the room. Then, cradling the little one in his arms, he said, "Whoever embraces one of these children as I do embraces me, and far more than me—God who sent me."

Mark 9:36–37

If the hospital environment is strange for you, imagine how it appears to a child. Put yourself in your child's place and view it with young and innocent eyes. That's what Angie did when her five-year-old son, Chandler, started chemo treatment in November of 2005.

Chandler was stripped down to his underwear, on his way to the bathtub, when the nurses came to give him a series of shots. Angie describes what her little boy saw. "They came in with five big needles and the chemo gear, which was a shield over their faces and great big gloves and the great big gown. They looked like aliens coming toward him."

Even though Angie is an experienced registered nurse, she began to cry. They told her to stop, but she said, "He's my son. He knows I cry. And, oh, I cried. He was this little child with these four nurses all dressed in this alien gear, coming at him and making him have pain."

Hopefully, your child's experience won't be as traumatic as Chandler's. Even so, the hospital is an alien world for your child. Look at it through his eyes: The room doesn't look like his bedroom at home. People in weird clothes use words or language he doesn't understand. He's surrounded by machines that look like something from a science fiction movie. And sometimes people do stuff that hurts even though they say it will make him feel better.

If you look at the hospital world with young eyes, you can empathize with your child, like Angie did. And more than that, you will recognize health care professionals—from doctors to nurses to technicians—who know how to talk to children and put them at ease.

That quality was evident in Dr. Ashcraft, one of our son's pediatric surgeons. When I asked him what his secret was, he said he talked to the children, not just to their parents. "You have to do that, no matter how old they are. You talk to them, you smile at them, you make faces and make them relax and grin if at all possible. And I've always loved children. I seem to have a knack for relating to kids."

When I asked the doctor how he reconciled his love for children with the need to inflict pain during treatment, he replied, "Well, somebody has to do it. And I figure it might as well be somebody who really likes them."

During this hospital stay, your little one will experience pain when in the hands of health care workers. As Dr. Ashcraft said, somebody has to do it. Your job as a parent is to ferret out the ones who genuinely like kids and make those people part of your child's treatment team.

Jenny, the young woman who survived childhood leukemia, says she realized how important that was, even as a child in the hospital. Her recommendation is pretty simple. "Find a doctor you can hug. Find somebody who can explain things to you in a way that's meaningful and understandable. Most people in the medical profession are good at that."

That's good news for you and your child. The alien world you inhabit today is unfamiliar, but it's also full of people who like kids, people God endowed to help your child. When they wrap their arms and hearts around a small body struggling to live, whether the health care workers believe in God or not, their hands will be the hand of Christ: a loving, familiar hand in an alien hospital world.

Father God, give me the eyes of a child so I can see the hospital from my child's point of view. Help me anticipate and quell fears before they begin. Lead me to health care workers you have prepared to love and respect my child. Show me how to make them part of my child's team.

Which nurses and doctors show genuine love and compassion to your child? How do you see the hand of Christ in their words and actions? What can you do to consistently involve those people in your child's treatment?

Take Time to Reflect

15

The Shirt Off Her Back

Every desirable and beneficial gift comes out
of heaven. The gifts are rivers of light cascad-
ing down from the Father of Light.

James 1:17

I was too shocked to thank the elderly woman who gave
me an unforgettable gift during Allen's first hospital stay. The
woman and her middle-aged son lived near the hospital. In
those pre-Ronald McDonald House days, they rented rooms
to parents like us. She was short and slight, with thin, papery
skin stretched over birdlike bones. Her son looked like Tim
Conway, but lacked the comedian's sense of humor.

Our landlady nodded when we left each morning and
asked about our baby when we returned each evening. Her
son, on the other hand, wasn't a big conversationalist. On

the morning Hiram told him we'd locked our keys in the car, the wordless gentleman grabbed a coat hanger and walked to the side of the street where we had parked. His mom tagged along.

Cars whizzed by as the pinch-faced landlord hunted for a place to slip the bent hanger through and pull up the lock button. But the large windows were shut tight. The fly window on the front passenger door was open a crack, but he couldn't generate enough upward pull to lift the lock button.

Hiram pushed the small window open as far as possible, stuck his hand in, and strained toward the button. But his arm, too wide for the opening, wouldn't quite reach. Our imitation Tim Conway, smaller than my husband, gave it a try. No go. Hiram turned to me. "Think you can reach it?" I tried, but even my arm was too wide. Right about then I succumbed to my inner panic, certain we would have to pay some locksmith to retrieve the keys, certain the breast milk I'd just pumped would go sour before it got to the hospital, certain I wouldn't see my baby that day.

Then our elderly landlady elbowed past me. "My arms are skinny. Let me try." She slid her arm through the window slot until her fingers were within millimeters of the lock button. Then she withdrew her wrinkled arm. "My shirt is in the way. I'll just take it off."

Before we could say a word, she whipped off her shirt, handed it to her son, and stuck a bare arm through the fly window. "But, Ma!" he protested. "Ma, put your shirt on. Ma!" He flapped his arms and turned in a circle.

74

His mother crammed her torso, clad only in a dingy brassier with elastic straps so old they fought a losing battle with gravity, against the car and reached for the button. Her fingertips brushed against it, but couldn't close around it.

"Ma!" Her son continued to turn in circles. "Put your shirt on, Ma."

"But I've almost got it."

"No, please," Hiram interrupted, his face flaming red. "Your son's right. Put on your shirt."

Finally she did put her shirt on, and her son took her by the arm. "One more try and I would have gotten it," I heard her mutter as her son pushed her across the lawn.

I don't remember how Hiram got the car unlocked. I was too shocked by the gift I received from an elderly mother who sensed my panic, my need to be with my son. In my shock, I forgot to tell her thank you. But I'm sure she knew I was grateful, because her son had been a baby once, too. That's why she gave me the shirt off her back.

Somewhere in your lonely hospital world, someone who understands your hurt is willing to give you the shirt off her back. And when the offer comes, I hope you recognize the source of such a sacrificial gift. It comes from the Father of Lights. He also has a Son—a Son who was a baby once, too.

Dear Father of Light, sometimes being in the hospital with my child makes me panic. I need evidence of your compassion so I can stay calm for my child. You know the gift I need. Please, I beg you, send it.

What hospital situations send you into panic mode? Why do they do that to you? What or who can help you stay calm?

Take Time to Reflect

16

What's Your Greatest Fear?

> "I'm leaving you well and whole. That's my
> parting gift to you. Peace. I don't leave you the
> way you're used to being left—feeling aban-
> doned, bereft. So don't be upset. Don't be
> distraught."
>
> John 14:27

Over the years, I've asked parents of sick children to name their greatest fears. Parents who have lost their only child fear childlessness. Parents of a dying child fear the pain their child will experience. Parents told their child has an 80 percent chance to live fear the 20 percent chance of death. Parents of children likely to survive fear their child will develop a victim mentality or suffer from posttraumatic stress.

When Naomi was told her toddler would die of brain cancer, her greatest fear was his fear of the unknown: death. "Joel used to watch *The Lion King* all the time before he got sick. So when he got sick, before he lost his speech, he asked me, 'Am I going to die like Mufasa?'"

Naomi did more than whisper reassuring, empty platitudes to Joel. She called Focus on the Family, a Christian organization headquartered in Colorado, and asked them to recommend children's books that dealt with heaven and death. A few days later, "a wonderful, gracious gift" arrived, a box of children's illustrated books. They answered many of Joel's questions, such as, "How do you get from earth to heaven? Who are the angels who are there for you?"

"We would sit and read the books together," says Naomi. "They gave him a lot of peace."

Listening to Naomi's story, I couldn't help but contrast her child-centered, logical way of dealing with her fears to my selfish, emotional responses. My fear-o-meter kicked into gear every time Allen entered the hospital. My emotional distress was heightened by a lethal combination: the actual hospital experience—beeping monitors, Code Blue announcements, doctors bustling by in white coats and pediatric nurses in scrubs printed with kid-friendly designs—mixed with a heavy dose of *General Hospital* unreality, compliments of several years of soap opera viewing. With my imagination working overtime, I was frequently trapped in a downward spiral of fear I could neither identify nor attack.

Though we had every assurance that our son would live and thrive once his anomalies were surgically corrected, I perceived life as a rabbit's warren of fears, which led to a nasty result. My preoccupation kept me from recognizing my son's fears and helping him through his struggles.

I wish I'd had Naomi's example to follow when my son was little, but I didn't. Throughout his childhood and adolescence, issues of abandonment and impulsiveness haunted Allen. When he was a young adult, therapy for medical-induced, posttraumatic stress syndrome brought him great peace. But until then, I wondered if my fears contributed to his struggle. Had I been calm instead of fearful during his hospitalizations, such guilt would not have plagued me.

My past can't be changed. But it can help you avoid the same trap. Now is the time to step back and examine your thoughts. Are you focused on your fears or your child's fears? Focus on your child's. Are the fears your child must confront real or imagined? Banish all but the real ones. Take a look at the ones that remain and do whatever is necessary to guide your child through them. Find books like Naomi did. Check out Web sites. Call a hotline. Seek the advice of your pastor. Ask the nurse to contact the hospital social worker or child life specialist and enlist their help.

God promises the gift of peace. You can take Him at His word, even during your child's hospital stay. Reach out and accept His gift. Unwrap it. Embrace it. And help your child embrace it, too.

Dear Father, I am struggling to overcome fear while my child lies in a hospital bed. I need your peace if I'm to be well and whole for my sick child. But I can't find peace on my own. Lead me to the peace you alone provide.

What are your fears for your child? What fears has your child expressed? Which are fears you can do something about? How will you begin to calm them?

Take Time to Reflect

17

Go Ahead and Laugh

A cheerful disposition is good for your health;
gloom and doom leave you bone-tired.

Proverbs 17:22

Susan, Allen's primary care nurse, met us at the NICU desk one day when he was about a week old. "He has a fever. He's not tolerating the formula feedings. Has your milk supply increased?"

"No." I shook my head. Since Allen's birth, I'd used a breast pump to make my milk come in, with limited success. The nurses eagerly poured the tiny amounts of breast milk I produced down Allen's feeding tube. My meager offerings were supplemented with formula to which, we'd begun to suspect, he was lactose intolerant. My baby's need for breast milk was urgent.

"If you want, the doctor can write a prescription for a nasal spray that triggers the let-down reflex," Susan suggested.

Desperate for a solution, I grabbed at her offer like a drowning woman thrown a life preserver. Susan hunted down the doctor and returned with the prescription. While we held and soothed our son, all I could think about was getting the prescription filled. As soon as we left the hospital, we drove through the dusky June twilight to the nearest drugstore. I prayed and fought tears the entire time. *God, let this work. Let this help our baby, please.*

I waited impatiently while the pharmacist filled the prescription, and snatched the bag from his hand while Hiram paid the bill. On the way back to the car, I ripped the package and pulled out the spray bottle. "Why don't you wait until we're in our room to use that?" Hiram suggested.

When I looked up to tell him in no uncertain terms, "There's no time to wait. Our baby needs my milk now, immediately, yesterday," a movement from the compact car next to ours caught my eye and my harsh, frantic words remained unspoken. "Look Hiram," I said and pointed at the car. A huge, furry sheepdog filled the front passenger seat. We both stared at Fido in the front seat. For some reason, the tableau was so comical we both started giggling, and I took pictures of this dead ringer for Disney's Shaggy Dog, choking with laughter, barely able to keep the camera from shaking. For the first time since being with Allen at the hospital, Hiram and I laughed together, wrapped in the joy of silliness.

Finally, we wiped our eyes, got into our car, and drove to our boarding house. As promised, the nasal spray triggered my let-down reflex, and that night I pumped six ounces of precious milk. From then on, my milk flowed freely and provided the nourishment and healing Allen needed.

Did God use the medicine to answer my desperate prayer? Or did our laughter outside the drugstore allow my body to relax and do what nature had prepared it to do? We'll never know. But I do know how good it felt to laugh and be silly for a short while. My ability to face our son's still precarious situation increased when laughter entered my emotional equation.

If you're sitting in a hospital with a sick child, worried and stressed, unable to relax, God knows you could use something to laugh about. He uses humor to revive your aching heart and prescribes laughter to trigger your relaxation reflex so you can comfort your child.

Ask the God who created laughter to inject some into your life today. When He answers your prayer, accept His prescription with a smile. Be silly for a few minutes. Giggle with your little one who needs to know it's okay to laugh in the hospital. Let your laughter be a joyful medicine for your child.

Go ahead and laugh.

Dear Father, I haven't laughed in a long time. Somehow, it doesn't seem right to laugh in the hospital where children are sick and dying. But you created laughter as a way to heal and relax. So bring us laughter as we sit in the hospital.

How has laughter reduced your stress level in the past? How could it do so during your child's hospital stay? What can you do to create laughter for your family?

Take Time to Reflect

18

They're People, Not Gods

> When the crowd saw what Paul had done, they
> went wild, calling out ... "The gods have come
> down! These men are gods!" ... When Barna-
> bas and Paul finally realized what was going
> on, they stopped them ... "What do you think
> you're doing? We're not gods! We are men just
> like you."
>
> Acts 14: 11–15

A doctor often holds the power of life and death in his skilled hands. But when parents pin all their hopes for their sick child on the ability of a gifted physician, they're one step away from viewing a human being as a god.

Chuck and Pat could have viewed their doctor that way. When their son Jason was born, his bowel and liver were outside his body, encased in a membrane where the umbilical cord attached to the body. Surgeons tried to put the organs inside his tiny body, but the liver pressed on Jason's heart and stopped it momentarily.

Pat described what the doctors did next. "They had his liver and bowel in a little baggie, tied up above him. The doctor compared the procedure to a toothpaste tube where they would gradually put a little bit in at a time, and gradually have his body get accustomed to it and have enough space for it."

But the procedure wasn't proven. The doctors only knew of three other babies who had survived it. And when Jason continued to bleed internally for a few days, the doctors doubted he could survive another surgery.

But one morning Dr. Hopkins, the surgeon, had good news for Chuck and Pat. "The bleeding has really slowed overnight. He's gotten a lot more stable. I'm willing to fight this if you are."

Dr. Hopkins held Jason's life in his hands. Although he's been in that position many times, he wants you to see doctors as people. "The expectations are much too high. Parents want a magical cure. There must be some way of communicating to them that they're not going to have a perfect child or a perfect result. Boy, that's a tough thing to know ahead of time. But I would find a way to get that attitude across at the beginning."

Dr. Hopkins conveyed his realistic attitude to Chuck and Pat. They trusted him with their child's life. But they also knew the doctor was human, one of the many people God, who alone holds life and death in His hands, used in Jason's life.

Dr. Jones, who practiced pediatric oncology for several years, shares a similar viewpoint. "Remember, your doctor is part of the team you are on in caring for your child. With chronic disease, you have a huge multidisciplinary team. I would get away from the pedestal approach because one, I knew I wasn't the expert, and two, in this day and age it's not realistic for one person to call the shots, because they won't know necessarily the best combination of things for each individual case."

Do you hear what these doctors are saying? They don't want to be viewed as gods. They want to be seen as skilled men and women who lend their expertise to the team caring for your child. And they want you to have realistic expectations of their abilities and limitations.

But don't beat yourself up when you're tempted to turn your doctor into a god. Throughout history, people have exalted the visible, physical creature over the invisible, spiritual creator whenever God uses men and women to reveal His healing power.

So when you catch yourself putting your doctor on a pedestal, remember what Dr. Jones said. You're as valuable a member of your child's health care team as the doctor is. But would you put yourself on a pedestal? No. Instead you ask God to work through you in your child's life. Because He's God, and you're not.

While you're at it, ask God to work through and in the doctor, too. After all, the doctor's a person in need of prayer, just like you.

Dear Father, it is so hard to trust the God I can't see when my child's life is at risk. It is so tempting to place my faith in the doctors and modern medicine instead of in the One who works through them. Give me eyes to see the doctors as people and you alone as God.

When is it hardest for you to trust the God you can't see? When are you tempted to put all your faith in doctors you can see? How can you keep from viewing the doctors treating your child as gods?

Take Time to Reflect

19

The Waiting Game

Meanwhile, friends, wait patiently for the Master's Arrival. You see farmers do this all the time, waiting for their valuable crops to mature, patiently letting the rain do its slow but sure work. Be patient like that. Stay steady and strong. The Master could arrive at any time.

James 5:7–8

To the passerby, I looked like any mother who'd spent the night in her child's hospital room. My hair stood on end; my clothes were wrinkled; my dragon breath was potent.

Beneath my slimy surface, I was engaged in a pastime that afflicts many impatient, worried hospital parents. I was playing the waiting game. The game varies from parent to parent, but over the years, my game went something like this.

Round #1

My sore, swollen chest reminded me it was time for the breast pump. But the nurse said the surgeon, along with his retinue of a half dozen medical students, was conducting rounds. Usually they arrived just after I hooked up my milking equipment, and I felt like a Jersey heifer strutting her stuff at the county fair. I was convinced the notes the doctors scribbled on their clipboards included, "Patient's mother is mentally unstable. She has a breast fetish." So I tried to wait until after rounds to pump. In the meantime, I crossed my arms over my chest and prayed that Allen's crying wouldn't trigger the let-down reflex until after the doctors left the room.

Round #2

My hair was greasy and an armpit sniff test made my eyes water. But the nurse said the doctor would arrive any minute. Hiram wasn't scheduled to relieve me for an hour, and since I wanted to ask the surgeon if the IV in Allen's foot could be removed, I waited for a shower until after my husband and/or the physician showed up.

Round #3

When our stomachs growled in unison, Hiram and I remembered we hadn't eaten since mid-morning. We were starving, so I volunteered to pick up supper from the cafeteria. But the nurse said a tech was coming to take Allen for an X-ray. We both wanted to go along to comfort him, so we waited and postponed supper until after the X-ray. By then the cafeteria was closed.

Maybe you've played the waiting game, too. Maybe you're playing it right now. You're waiting for someone to come or for something to happen. You're impatient and worried, fretting as you wait. If you're like me, this life-on-hold frustrates you because you've never learned to wait. The only reason you're waiting is because you have to, not because you're practicing the art of patience. But true waiting requires true patience, and that's not something anyone in our click-and-find-it, instant gratification culture practices very often.

In the New Testament, the writer of the book of James tells us to be patient, like farmers waiting for the rain, when living through events we can't control. He encourages us to develop patience by waiting for what we can't see, but for what God promises will come. So farmers wait for rain, and people who believe in Jesus wait for the coming of the Lord. As the parent of a sick child, you're waiting for something unseen, too. Right now, you probably don't have a clue of what it might be.

My husband and I waited over twenty years for God to completely heal our son. Last year, when Allen and I returned to the motel after his fourth day of a week-long, intensive outpatient treatment for posttraumatic stress syndrome, he sighed as we entered our motel room. "For the first time in my life, I have peace," he said. "The internal noise is gone, and I know how to control it when it starts again."

I wrapped his broad shoulders in a grateful embrace and thanked God for granting His patience during the long years of waiting.

"For the first time in my life, I have peace."

Those words were worth the wait.

Dear Father, there are moments and hours and days when I don't think I can wait any longer. And yet, as long as my child is in this hospital, I have to wait. Teach me patience, Lord. Teach me to wait for you to fulfill your unseen promises, no matter how long it takes.

When is waiting hardest for you? What gives you strength to wait during those times?

Take Time to Reflect

20

An Educated Advocate

Wise men and women are always learning,
always listening for fresh insights.

Proverbs 18:15

During my interviews with parents familiar with pediatric illness, one question always received a lengthy response: Do you have any advice for parents about how to be an advocate for your hospitalized child? Parents have plenty to say about the importance of advocacy, and their suggestions are based on their firsthand experiences.

Dave and Christy became parent advocates when their seven-year-old son AJ was diagnosed with Crohn's, a chronic, inflammatory bowel disease. Dave says all his efforts begin with prayer. Otherwise, "I begin to rely on myself and how I can make this work. I forget where the strength and power come from. I think that's the first part of it. But certainly," Dave continues, "be educated. I'd never heard of Crohn's disease before. I wanted to be educated about it so I could speak intelligently, ask intelligent questions."

Christy is a physician's assistant. Her training, combined with her experience as the parent of a child with a chronic condition, gives her a unique perspective. "Asking questions is really important, being prepared and educated. You have to be your child's advocate. One thing I've learned as a health care provider is that parents know their children best. If the parents say, 'Something is wrong,' they're usually right. I would tell parents to trust that, and to go after it."

Dave adds that finding the right doctor is crucial. "When you're dealing with a chronic illness, this is going to be your child's doctor for his whole childhood and beyond. So find a doctor you can communicate with well."

Christy agrees. "You need to go where you're comfortable, where you feel you're getting your questions answered."

Dr. Hopkins, a pediatric surgeon, says it's a challenge for doctors to provide parents with all the treatment options, and differing opinions about them, in a short amount of time. But, he says, "You shouldn't withhold information, even if you think it's way above someone's head. They may be able to deal with it."

Christy has some final advice for parents who have had well-meaning people tell them that using modern medical technology indicates a lack of faith. "God has given the brains and the expertise to the physicians that have created these medications. It would be irresponsible for me to say, 'I'm not going to take AJ to his next treatment because I just think I'm just going to trust God.' I understand the disease process, and I think it's imperative to take the medication that the doctors tell you to take."

Dave, Christy, and Dr. Hopkins want you to know that no matter how old you are or what your level of formal schooling might be, you can become an educated advocate. You can learn about your child's illness. You can ask good questions and understand the answers. You're already your child's most passionate advocate. You have what it takes to become a well-educated one, too.

Dave told you what he did: All his efforts to educate himself began with prayer. And Christy reminds you that the God who gave the physicians brains and expertise to develop modern medical technology is the same God who gave you the brains necessary to learn about your child's illness. Even though you're sitting in a hospital, you have everything you need to begin.

So start praying and start learning. You can become the advocate your child needs.

Dear Father of wisdom, I never thought I would have to be this kind of advocate for my child. I'm not sure I can understand the medical terms the doctor uses. But I am sure that my child needs an educated advocate. So open my mind and teach me.

What things don't you understand about your child's condition and treatment? What questions can you have ready to ask the next time you see the doctor? Is there a library for parents in the hospital or wireless Internet available so you can do further research?

Take Time to Reflect

Conflicting Dreams

Juggling Two Worlds

21

Juggling Two Worlds

So speak encouraging words to one another.
Build up hope so you'll all be together in this,
no one left out, no one left behind. I know
you're already doing this; just keep on doing it.

1 Thessalonians 5:11

I'm not much of a juggler. Tossing one ball back and forth in gym class was a challenge for me. Keeping track of two or three was impossible. I wasn't any better at juggling the increased responsibilities of motherhood after Allen was born. I could handle parenting when my only task was to concentrate on his needs. But when my teaching job resumed three months later, I had difficulty coordinating work and Allen's care.

We had enjoyed six weeks of normal babyhood with Allen after his release from NICU. But at two months of age, he needed a second life-saving surgery due to unexpected complications. For several months after that, his recovery depended upon special care, and he received all his feedings through a stomach tube. Since breast milk was the only food he could tolerate, I pumped four times—at home, at school, in the middle of the night—every day.

Three times a week, we left the house at 5:30 AM and made the 240-mile round trip from Camp Crook to Rapid City with a very hungry baby strapped into his car seat. He couldn't eat from midnight until after an 8:00 AM endoscopy procedure. On the days we weren't in Rapid City, the blessed normal days, we went to our jobs and left Allen in the care of a sitter who cuddled him by the hour and wasn't scared of his feeding tube.

My first two months at work were consumed by my frantic attempts at juggling doctor's appointments, sorting and paying mountains of bills, teaching school, and mothering our baby.

Everything came crashing down on Halloween when the sitter called me at school just before noon. "Allen's tube looks funny. And he's throwing up. Can you come over during your lunch hour?"

Before I left, I told the other teachers, "I'll be back for the afternoon. I can't be gone for the Halloween party."

Karen, the special education tutor and mother of two of my students, put her hands on my shoulders. "I'll take care of the party, Jolene. Take your son to the doctor if you need to." She hugged me close while I cried. "It's okay." She rubbed my back. "We'll get you through this." Then she pushed me out the door.

She was one of the many people in our tiny town who had rallied around us since Allen's birth. During his hospitalizations, friends and neighbors cared for our garden, mowed our lawn, cleaned the house, and filled the freezer. Once we came home, our bosses were accommodating and supportive. People gave us money. Substitute teachers came out of the woodwork.

Because our friends and neighbors loved us and our son, they refused to let us juggle normal life and the hospital world alone. Through the people in our town, God taught us a lesson I want to share with you.

People are watching you juggle your job, your family responsibilities at home, and the needs of your sick child. They know you can't do it alone. They want to help. God calls them to help. He's brought them to you and wants you to relinquish everything they can juggle for you. He wants you to concentrate on the things only you can keep in the air.

That's what Karen did for me on the day of the Halloween party. And she was right. My students survived without me. In fact, they had a great time while my husband and I spent the weekend in the hospital parenting our son and plying a breast pump, the responsibilities only we could juggle.

Father, I am exhausted from trying to juggle too many things during my child's illness. Give me wisdom to see what you want me to concentrate on and what I can pass on to others. Make me humble enough to admit my weaknesses and accept help.

What are the responsibilities you are juggling right now? Which are the ones no one but you can handle? Which ones can you pass on to someone else? How will you begin to accomplish that?

Take Time to Reflect

22

All in the Family

A good life gets passed on to the
grandchildren.

Proverbs 13:22

With your life bouncing back and forth between the real world and the hospital world, it's tempting to neglect extended family. Sometimes their concern for your child is so draining, you wonder if you have the emotional strength to deal with their worries. Keeping them informed about the illness of their grandchild, niece, nephew, or cousin drains your precariously low reservoirs of time and energy.

But in most cases, if you neglect those family ties, you and your child will lose out on an important source of strength and support. Even though your family members' desire to be involved in your child's hospitalization

103

can sometimes exhaust or distract you, their love for your youngster nearly matches your own. Not only that, but by God's design they are your strongest allies and your most passionate champions. They will come to your aid, no matter where, no matter when.

Angie said that's what her dad, Curt, did for her and Chandler. After his leukemia diagnosis in November, Chandler's condition was declining rapidly at the hospital in Rochester, Minnesota. His temperature was 104 degrees, he was on morphine, and he had developed pressure sores because he was so thin. "Everything hurt so bad," Angie remembers. "That was the night my dad was out on the combine ... I would call his cell phone and he would answer and I would just start to cry."

It was the middle of harvest, and Curt, a Minnesota farmer, was combining corn, but he became her passionate champion right where he was. "Well, Angie," he told her, "let me see what I can do here. I need to get some people over there with you."

Curt knew their former pastor had recently moved to Rochester, and to get in contact with her, for the next few hours Curt made call after call. "He went through I don't know how many numbers to get our pastor's number from his cell phone on the combine," says Angie. At midnight, the pastor walked into Chandler's room. This time, Angie cried tears of relief.

Extended family members want to support parents and their sick child even though they are grieving about the situation. Jeff and Carolyn's parents were a huge support to them during their daughter Beth's long illness. They were very involved and visited their granddaughter and Carolyn in the hospital and at home often. Even so, Carolyn said she thought Beth's illness was harder on the grandparents than it was on them. "Because we were right there. And when you experience the thing with the person who's going through it, it's easier to know exactly what's going on and how they're feeling."

Think of that. Your child's illness can be harder on the people who aren't there because they don't share the first-hand experience. If that's true, no wonder Curt made all those phone calls from the seat of his combine. No wonder Jeff and Carolyn's family were at the hospital as often as possible. No wonder your family members are anxious and beg you to call with updates.

God designed your family to passionately love your child. He designed them to love you. By seeing the situation from their point of view, you can help them better deal with their worries. You can let them into your struggle, even if it means a little more juggling on your part. Your family needs to be involved. Your child needs their support.

So do you. Because when you reach your lowest point, it's someone in your family who will answer your frantic, midnight phone call. And while the sound of that familiar voice brings you to tears, it can also reassure you. For only that voice can speak the words you are longing to hear. "Honey, let me see what I can do. I need to get some people there with you."

Dear Father, my extended family members need to know what's happening with my child. But when I hear their familiar voices, tears will flow. Give me energy to meet their needs and to ask them to be our passionate champions.

Why might you be reluctant to keep your extended family up-to-date about your child's condition? What needs do they have that you are too tired to address? How can your family help you in ways no one else can?

Take Time to Reflect

23

Two Families Are Better Than One

Stay on good terms with each other, held together by love. Be ready with a meal or a bed when it's needed. Why, some have extended hospitality to angels without ever knowing it!

Hebrews 13:1–2

Your extended family can be a great support to you while you juggle life inside and outside the hospital, but they can't be your only support. Your child's circumstances are too big for them to shoulder alone because they're too close to what's happening to your child.

Think of your present medical situation as a target. Your child is the center. As parents, you're in the first ring surrounding the center. Extended family occupies the next ring. The outer ring includes close friends, co-workers, and your church family, if you have one. You need the support of the people in that outer ring, the people who have a little less emotional attachment than those near the center, but with plenty of compassion and practical love.

When Curt couldn't come to Angie and Chandler, who did he call? Their pastor. And because the pastor was slightly removed from the situation, she could help Angie sort through what was happening. "She came walking into the room, and it was just like an angel. She opened the door, and it was light shining from behind her."

Then Angie asked a hard question. "How can God be in control of this? How can a child who is six years old lay here on a morphine drip?"

The pastor answered with compassion. "He's not only in control; He's right here beside the bed weeping with you."

The pastor's answer changed the way Angie saw God. "He's not standing there saying, 'All right, you're going to have this—now, deal with it.' But He's going through the circumstances with us, and He's crying with us when we cry."

Members of a church family can answer hard questions, and they can do much more. Dave and Christy said their church family showed them how believers bear one another's burdens. One woman from their church, a total stranger, saw their son's name on a prayer sheet and stopped in to visit because she worked near the hospital.

People helped in other ways, too. "We'd come home and someone would show up with a meal. With our two other kids at home, we'd take turns at the hospital, so not having to cook was a blessing," Dave said.

Naomi said their church family was amazing during Joel's struggle with brain cancer. "They upheld us in prayer. Financially, they gave money to the point where we hardly had anything to pay for ourselves. They helped us in every way. They were encouragers."

You need encouragers. So reach out to your church family, if you have one, and ask them to help. If the nasty voices in your head say you shouldn't ask because your family isn't actively involved in your church, ignore them. God created the body of believers to be the practical supporters and encouragers in times like these.

Expect the love of your church family to change you. Someday, your child's present medical situation will end. And someday, maybe soon or maybe years from now, you will be ready to bear the burdens of other parents who are hurting. The kindness of God's people extended to you will make you sensitive to the needs of others in your church family. Someday, when you're healed and whole, you'll be the one who visits the hospital, brings meals, and prays for others.

But for now, let your church family do what they were created to do: bear your burdens, offer a bed, make a meal.

Let them be the evidence of a God who cries with you and your child.

Dear God who cries, thank you for weeping with me. Thank you for providing people to dry my tears. Thank you for creating a church family to bear our family's burdens.

How can your church family best support you? Who can you contact so your needs will be communicated to your church family? If you don't have a church family, can the hospital chaplain connect you to a church?

Take Time to Reflect

24

She Doesn't Go Away

> But Ruth said, "Don't force me to leave you; don't make me go home. Where you go, I go; and where you live, I'll live ... so help me God—not even death itself is going to come between us!"
>
> Ruth 1:16–17

Having a sick child creates a great deal of stress. And if the illness is serious enough for your attention to be divided between hospital life and home life for an extended period of time, the stress can attack the fabric of a marriage and unravel it.

Travis and Jamie said that's what happened to them after their three-year-old son was originally diagnosed with Stage IV neuroblastoma in 1996. Nic's treatment, which included chemo; radiation; an eleven-hour, tumor-debunking surgery; and a bone marrow transplant, was immediate and aggressive. It turned their normal lives upside down.

Travis says that back then, their marriage wasn't as strong as it is now, and their relationship went into a tailspin. "I think Jamie wanted to be my support. She would have been if I had let her. But I didn't let anybody be my support the first time. I was just mad. We didn't communicate on anything other than what was going on with Nic."

Jamie was in a difficult spot. "I was so busy … I didn't have a choice. I didn't have a chance to deal with it. I just had to take care of Nic."

Nic's bone marrow transplant was performed more than two hours away from home. Jamie and her son lived in the hospital the first month and in the Ronald McDonald House for a second month. "Travis would come over on the weekends. He would bring models, and he and Nic would play games."

"We'd be in the same room," Travis says, describing the atmosphere between him and Jamie. "We'd try to get along, but there was just too much tension. I mean, we were never angry with each other, but we just didn't connect."

Their marriage seemed to be over. When Nic's treatment ended, Jamie and Nic moved to her parents' home in Minnesota. The preschooler spent several months recovering from the transplant, and Jamie healed from the trauma of caring for a child with cancer. Travis came up on the weekends to be with Nic. And it was during those visits, Jamie says, that somehow they fixed things. Eventually, Jamie and Nic moved home again.

With a sense of wonder, Travis and Jamie talk about how they stitched their marriage back together. Jamie looks at Travis and smiles. "You didn't know how to handle yourself. You didn't know how to get help to handle it. You weren't a bad person. You wanted to be there for us. You just didn't know how."

"You know," Travis says, his eyes on Jamie, "in a way Nic's illness saved our marriage. Because we realized we are there for each other. A lot of it was just realizing there's somebody there who cares about me ... She doesn't go away when things are rough."

If the strain of illness and hospital life is unraveling your marriage, let Travis and Jamie's story provide a tiny thread of hope. Jamie didn't leave when things were rough. She did remove herself from the situation so she and Nic could heal, but she didn't leave Travis stranded. And he didn't abandon his family. He spent time with his son while Jamie healed.

Your family has endured a great trauma. Your child isn't the only one who needs to heal. God knows that you, your spouse, and your marriage need healing, too. He knows that when this crisis is over, you both need time to think and forgive and to be forgiven. So take the time you need and ask God to repair the fabric of your relationship and to make it even stronger.

Dear Father, this illness has been hard on our marriage. We're under so much stress, I worry it will unravel. Show me how to forgive and be forgiven. Show me how to communicate. Show me when to step back and give our marriage time to heal.

What stresses has this hospital stay put on your marriage? How well are you and your spouse able to communicate? In what ways can you offer forgiveness and space so you, your spouse, and your marriage can heal? Have you asked the chaplain, social worker, or doctor about counseling resources where you live?

Take Time to Reflect

25

Start Talking

Be gracious in your speech.
The goal is to bring out the best in others in a
conversation, not put them down, not cut
them out.

Colossians 4:6

Travis and Jamie's story illustrates the difficulties of juggling marriage and life as hospital parents. But if you're a parent who is already separated or divorced, you face a different challenge. How do you and your child's other parent put your differences aside and create a united team to support your child?

Angie describes how hard it was for her and Greg, Chandler's dad. "We had tried to reconcile after our divorce, so we had been together for about a year, and it had only been about six weeks since we had separated when Chandler got sick. So it was very volatile. We were trying to blame each other for what was happening."

Greg is a good dad to Chandler. "He was very involved," says Angie. "But I think he couldn't handle it and pulled away. I don't think I understood what he needed to do at the time. So to let the other parent have their space to cope, in whatever way he needs to cope, I think is really important. 'Cause not everybody deals with illness in the same way."

Greg and Angie didn't talk about what was happening. And the big loser, Angie says, was their son. It didn't take Chandler long to realize Mom and Dad would both stand on their heads if he wanted them to. "He learned kind of how to play us against each other." And parents know that's not good for a sick child, or a healthy one, for that matter.

Dr. Hopkins, a pediatric surgeon, also stresses how important it is for parents to talk to one another and to other family members, as well as to the physicians, nurses, and other caregivers. "The main thing is to keep the lines of communication open, so the patients, parents, and their other family members do not feel isolated and withdraw. It is very important for parents to feel comfortable in expressing their concerns to each other and in asking for explanations and answers of their child's caregivers."

Talking to one another, whatever the state of your relationship may be, will keep you from withdrawing, from pulling away from your child's other parent. Your unity and cooperation are extremely important to your child's emotional and physical health.

But how do you talk to each other without every discussion becoming heated and angry? Pat, whose marriage survived years of surgery for one child and the death of another, shares a technique that aided communication between her and Chuck, her husband. "You should always have somebody else with you when doctors and nurses are telling you things, perhaps one of your parents or a trusted friend. Because we'd get in the car to come home and he'd have heard one thing and I'd have heard the other. I just don't think when you're emotional and worried that you hear everything." She continues. "I think you should always have an advocate there. Being able to talk about all that is important. It helps you come up with questions."

Sure, it will take some time to locate a neutral person who can bridge your communication gap. But finding the right person is as important to your youngster's emotional well-being as medical treatment is for his or her physical health. Someone in your family or a friend may be qualified and willing to fulfill the role. Also, the hospital chaplain or social worker can point you to organizations and people who can help.

The God who is present with you and your child in this hard time is a God of unity. No matter what differences people have, He calls them to lay them aside and move forward in love on behalf of the needy and the weak. If your child is seriously ill, needy and weak, God is calling you to this very task. So put aside your differences. Unite on behalf of your child. Find someone to help you. Start talking.

Dear Father, sometimes I have a hard time communicating with my child's other parent, even when things are going well. Under these strained circumstances, it seems impossible. But our child needs support from both of us. Please provide a way for us to communicate. Help us start talking.

Why is it important for you to communicate with your child's other parent? What are you afraid will happen when you try to talk to each other? What safeguards do you need to put in place so you can communicate in a healthy way?

Take Time to Reflect

26

Hush, Hug, Here

I've kept my feet on the ground,
   I've cultivated a quiet heart.
Like a baby content in its mother's arms,
   my soul is a baby content.

Psalm 131:2

Shhh ... be quiet, lie still. I'm here." How often have you whispered those words to your sick child recently? No matter what my son's age during a hospitalization–newborn, two months, two years, five or fifteen–at some point I rocked his small body, patted his bottom, touched his soft hair, or rubbed his cheek, and whispered, "Shhh, Allen. Be quiet. Lie still."

Often my words seemed hypocritical. Being continually yanked with my child from home to hospital and back again disrupted my equilibrium and sent my emotions spinning. In such an agitated state of mind, how could I tell my hurting son to be quiet and rest when I couldn't be still myself? How could my restless presence be his comfort?

Sometimes, however, I sensed God whispering those same words to me while I rocked my son. "Shhh … Jolene. Be quiet. Lie still. I'm here." In those moments, I wanted to crawl into His lap, feel His gentle arms around me, and be comforted while I grieved my son's loss of another day of good health and my loss of another day of normal life: trick-or-treating on his first Halloween, pushing his stroller around the block, playing peek-a-boo in the evening.

At the time, I didn't know I was grieving. Grief, I thought, was reserved for parents who lost their children. As the parent of a child who would someday be healthy again, this was ground I thought I was not allowed to tread. But I was wrong.

Chuck and Pat addressed this common misconception. "At some point, you do have to grieve and you do have to face what's happened, whether it's your child living, but not healthy the way you always dreamed … or if you actually lost your child. Whether you admit it or not, you are grieving, and you have to be able to reach out and talk to people."

Pat's words were a great comfort to me. I'd spent years pooh-poohing my pain, chiding myself for my drama queen emotions each time we took Allen to the hospital. What a relief to realize that while my grief over the loss of normal life was not the grief of losing a child, it was legitimate. It was real.

Jeff, who lost his daughter Beth many years ago, further legitimized grief for small things. He facilitates a counseling class for classroom teachers. "We spend half a day talking about how students are sad. They have fathers in Iraq. Or a bunch of kids are sad because their brother or sister went off to college. Or it can be something as simple as losing the football game Friday night."

Or, I thought, it could be something as small as spending Allen's first Halloween in the hospital instead of trick-or-treating in our neighborhood.

Then Jeff shared advice he'd received from one of the participants in his class, a pastor. When he ministers to people who are grieving, he practices the Three H's: Hush, Hug, and Here.

"Isn't that cool?" Jeff asked me." "Hush. Hug. Here. Be quiet, give your hug or form of showing you care, and then just hang out."

Your grief over your losses, no matter how small, is real. Allow yourself time to mourn them. Talk about your grief with people who practice the Three H's. Hush. Hug. Here.

God knows your child isn't the only one who needs comfort today. You do, too.

Shhh ... be quiet, lie still. Listen to Him whisper. *I'm here.*

Dear Father, quiet my soul. Whisper to my heart, touch me with your hand and be present with me as I grieve for the small things lost today. Hush me. Hug me. Be here with me.

What small things are you grieving for today? Who will listen to you talk about them? Who practices the Three H's in your life?

Take Time to Reflect

27

Homeless Wanderers

"Everything comes from you; all we're doing is
    giving back what comes from your generous
    hand.
As far as you're concerned, we're homeless,
    shiftless wanderers ... "

1 Chronicles 29:14–15

While your child is undergoing medical treatment,
your schedule can become an endless shuttling between
home and the clinic, home and the hospital, home and outpatient treatment, home and physical therapy. At worst, you
feel like a hamster running in circles; at best, like a wanderer
without an itinerary or destination. Yet often, God uses your
travels to connect you with people, and those people will

assist you during your child's medical journey—and perhaps even stick around once it's over.

God brought one such person into Jenny's life when she was a preschooler in the late 1980s. She and her mom were flying from North Dakota to Omaha, Nebraska, for one of her many chemotherapy treatments. "Apparently I had been pestering her about wanting to see how planes work. So my mom asked the flight attendant, and the flight attendant went in and talked to the pilot."

The Continental pilot, Pete, invited them into the cockpit and asked why they were on the plane. When he learned Jenny had cancer, he asked for the little girl's address. Her mom, though hesitant at first, could tell he was genuine and gave him the information. "Ever since that time, he's kept in touch with me, came to my high school graduation. He was there for me and supported my family and always sent me birthday cards."

Pete provided more than moral support. Through him, Jenny's family learned of an organization supported by the wives of Continental Airlines pilots. This group of women helped pay for plane tickets to get Jenny to treatments and check-ups. "I don't think Mom knew about that before meeting him … and once my whole three years of pretty aggressive chemotherapy treatment started, that kind of information just fell into place."

Pete came into Jenny's life while she and her mom were traveling. He stayed in her life long after her treatment ended, long after she was declared cancer-free. His presence was a great encouragement to Jenny and her family, visible proof of God's presence during her treatment journey.

Pete was engaged in his own travels when he met Jenny and her mom. Not a medical pilgrimage, but a journey nonetheless. And Jenny's presence brought meaning and focus to his trek.

We're all on some sort of journey. We all seek direction and resources as we wander through life. Most of the time we convince ourselves—or try to convince ourselves--that we're in charge of the itinerary and destination. But because of your child's illness, you know you're not in charge of the trip. You don't get to plan the itinerary. You don't know where you're going. And you don't know who will accompany you along the way.

But God will use your travels and the people you meet along the way to show you more of who He is. You'll discover He is in control of both your journey and its purpose. He's in control of your destination and everything you need along the way. And He'll use the people you meet to provide the resources for your journey. Even more amazing, though you feel blind and clueless, He'll use you to meet the needs of some other traveler on some other journey when your paths cross.

Jenny learned this truth during her medical travels. "There are people out there that'll help," she says. "I'm a product of that. I'm a reality of that. There are actually a lot of good people."

And one of them, Jenny knows, is named Pete.

Dear Father, thank you for watching over us on this journey. I feel like a homeless wanderer, but you have a destination and purpose for me and my child. Thank you for the people we will meet on this journey. Help me give to them as much as they give to us.

When have you felt like a homeless wanderer? How has God shown you He is in control? How have you and your child helped someone you've met along the way?

Take Time to Reflect

28

Life in the Pits

Bless the Lord, O my soul ...
Who redeems your life from the pit,
Who crowns you with lovingkindness and com-
   passion.

Psalm 103:2, 4 (NASB)

Hiram and I moved from one lodging to another during Allen's NICU stay. First there was the boardinghouse where the landlady gave us the shirt off her back. Then my sister called and said her in-laws, about thirty miles outside the city, would put us up. That was cheaper than the boardinghouse, and since everyone kept their clothes on, held fewer surprises; but the commute was long and tiring. So when Mom called with news that old family friends, a couple in an Omaha suburb, wanted us to stay with them, we moved again.

The moment we set foot in Dean and Johnny's house, it felt like home. Dean carried our suitcases to the basement bedroom. "Once you're settled in, come upstairs if you like. My wife made dessert."

We liked, and moments later Johnny greeted us in the kitchen with a hug. "Before you sit down," she said, "you have to sign the wall."

"Sign the wall?" Hiram and I spoke in unison.

"Not the wall," Johnny clarified. "The wallpaper." She pointed at the soffit above the stove. "The last owners put up this hideous fake brick wallpaper, and when we first moved in, we didn't have time to tear it down. So we decided that instead of having houseguests sign a guestbook, we'd have them sign a brick." She pulled over a chair and handed Hiram a marker. "Now we can't take the wallpaper down. Too many memories."

Both of us grinned and signed our names. But the fun was just beginning. Johnny served dessert at the dining room table. We enjoyed the sun flooding through the sliding doors that opened onto their backyard. Our hosts asked question after question about Allen and oohed over his picture. Suddenly, Johnny leapt to her feet. "He's back. I'm gonna show him." She snatched a slingshot from the counter, loaded it with something from a nearby bowl, opened the sliding door, and fired at a small tree. "Drat!" She slid the door shut. "I missed."

"Johnny's got an apricot war going with the squirrel in the backyard." Dean chuckled.

"Last year," Johnny interrupted, "the tree I planted was finally going to bear fruit. But the blasted squirrel ate every last apricot. All he left behind were the pits." She set down the slingshot and picked up the bowl beside it. "So I decided to show him. I bought a slingshot, and now I use the pits as ammunition."

Dean stood and took our plates. "Unfortunately, her aim isn't very good."

"Give me time." Johnny's eyes gleamed. "Just give me time."

We stayed with Dean and Johnny for the rest of Allen's NICU stay and again during his July and August hospitalizations. The days in the hospital were the pits, but the evenings were delightful. Over and over Johnny redeemed bad situations and unfortunate circumstances by finding the humor in them, by using them for good purposes. Her attitude was infectious. I began to look for ways God was redeeming Allen's hospitalization and our circumstances for good. Our friendship with Dean and Johnny was the first of many I experienced.

God can redeem your circumstances for good, too. That may seem unlikely to you, especially if your child's situation is deteriorating. But don't give up. Ask God to take your hardship and sadness and use them for good. He can and will redeem your life, and your child's, from the pits.

Dear Redeeming God, I don't see much good in this situation. But you promise to bring good from evil. You promise to redeem my family from this pit if I ask. Give me strength to hang on until your redemption is complete.

What circumstances in your present situation do you think are beyond redemption? How have you seen God redeem other situations you thought were hopeless? Are you ready to trust Him to bring good from this bad situation?

Take Time to Reflect

29

The Small Things

For who has despised the day of small things?
Zechariah 4:10 (NASB)

When your child is very sick, your days are packed with big things. One day, you make decisions that affect your family members' lives. The next day, you get news that either renews or dashes hope. Parenting becomes huge, dramatic, larger-than-life. Because the stakes are so high, your inclination is to ask God for guidance.

Once the crisis fades, however, it's hard to keep God in the everyday parenting picture. But that's what you have to do, whether your child is completely cured or a serious or chronic condition persists. As you transition from parenting in the hospital to parenting at home, your situation will be similar to every other parent's in at least one way. Most days, you will discover, are a series of responses to the small things in life. And the way you juggle the small things changes your child's world. That world is bigger, more purposeful and less stressful if you acknowledge God, even in the small things.

Doug and Brenda learned to make God part of the small things after their son Jeff was born with severe physical and mental limitations. When their daughter Jessica was born two years later with less serious physical disabilities and no mental issues, Brenda's life revolved around taking care of two babies who couldn't walk. "I was focused on their problems, and probably never looked beyond that little circle." She could handle the little things, but when the surgeries came along, she experienced a great deal of stress.

Doug was the opposite. He went to work each day and took time off to stay with the kids in the hospital. But when he was at home, surrounded by the small things, his frustration level was high. Slowly, he learned to cope with the small things. "As my faith has matured, it's allowed me to step back from those small things and look at the world in a different perspective. I don't have any control over anything to speak of … God has control over it. And I've got to learn to step back and allow that to happen and to not let the little things bug me, but control the things I'm supposed to control."

Doug and Brenda realized they weren't in control of the big things and left them with God. They concentrated on handling the small things they could control in ways that kept God in the picture. Their approach changed the way they lived. Brenda explained. "People are watching how we cope and handle things. We're supposed to be light. It's not about me anymore. It's not about my problems. It's about God and what He wants. That's been the evolution. A long one. A very long one."

Their frustration decreased when they stepped back and put the small things within the bigger picture of God's plan for their lives and the lives of their children. The same thing can happen to you, too. The change won't be quick and it won't be easy, but it's still worth doing, because your child's world matters, and the way you respond to the small things affect that world.

So turn to God with the big things: death, life, and illness. And turn to Him with the small things, too. On every ordinary day, turn over to God the things you can't control. Then take up the handful of small things that remain and deal with them, and keep God in the picture while you do. Because the small things matter. Even in the small things, you can be light.

Dear Father, how do I move from huge hospital decisions to everyday parenting? How do I sort through the big things you control and the small things you want me to handle? Grant me healthy respect for the small things. Show me how to respond to them in a way that pleases you.

What are the things you can't control in your present situation? What are the things you can and should control? How can you respond to them in a way that keeps God in the picture?

Take Time to Reflect

30

Separation Anxiety

Who will separate us from the love of Christ?
Romans 8:35 (NASB)

Good-bye, Annie." I kissed my daughter. "You be good, okay?"

Anne nodded. "Bye, Mommy. Bye, Allen."

"Bye, Annie." Abandoning his teen cool, her brother hugged her close. Then we slid across the icy driveway to the car.

Grandma and Anne waved from the door. I swallowed tears, aware of a grace I hadn't fully appreciated when our firstborn was a baby. No anxiety about neglected siblings, abandoned by their parents and missing their brother, haunted us during Allen's early, most critical years. We devoted ourselves to him wholeheartedly.

Now, after a ten-year hiatus, he faced another major surgery due to unexpected complications. So I left my daughter, knowing I would miss her third grade Christmas program, which was the same day as Allen's surgery. My heart was torn as the guilt of leaving her battled with the need to care for our son for the next few weeks.

Our family experienced this situation only once. I think that's why God packed it with complications, so I would appreciate families who regularly endure hospital separations.

The night before we were to leave for the hospital in Kansas City, my husband mentioned his sore throat. By morning, this man of steel who never gets sick spiked a temperature of 102. Allen and I made the four-hour trip to the hospital without Hiram—through an ice storm.

Things got worse. The day of Allen's surgery, Hiram's fever was so high that when I called with updates, he couldn't understand me. Grandma got Anne to her Christmas program, but the camera didn't work. Once Hiram's fever broke and he came to Kansas City, Grandma got sick. Anne moved in with family friends, the Smiths. Then Anne got sick. Then the Smiths got sick. My guilt and anxiety escalated.

If you have more than one child, you know this feeling. Whether it's happened to you once or it's an ongoing part of your family life, the needs of your healthy children war with those of your hospitalized child. You're so haunted by anxiety and guilt that you can't care for your sick child with an undivided heart.

Wholeness eluded me during our complication-packed separation. But Naomi, a friend of mine, remained calm under difficult circumstances with her son Joel. Duke University Hospital offered the only hope of a cure for her son's brain cancer. So Naomi spent six months with Joel, half a continent away from her two daughters and husband. When the treatment didn't work, she brought Joel home to die.

"It was hard," Naomi told me. "Our baby daughter was four months old when I left, and when I came back she was taking her first steps ... She didn't know who I was. Our older daughter, Jesse, was angry at me because I was gone so long and her brother disappeared. But I had to focus on the task ahead of me, and that's just the way it was. You're not the only person in the world who can provide your other children with love and affection and watch over them. Trust those you love to love them until you get through it."

I shared Naomi's story with Anne, now nineteen. "How did you feel when we missed your Christmas program and didn't get any pictures?"

"Was that the time I stayed with the Smiths?"

I nodded and held my breath.

She smiled. "I don't remember the Christmas program. But I had a blast at the Smiths. Besides," she added, "I knew you loved me."

Finally, every vestige of guilt and anxiety disappeared. And I thanked God for a second grace I hadn't fully appreciated at the time: the grace of friends who loved my daughter for me until our separation was over.

Dear Father, I can't be in two places at once. I want to be home with my other children, but I need to be here with my sick one. Assure my absent children of my love through the love of those who are caring for them. Though separated in body, unite us in your love.

What makes you feel guilty or anxious at being separated from your children? Who do you trust to care for and love your children in your absence?

Take Time to Reflect

The Unending Dream

Long-Term Health Conditions

31

The New Normal

The Enthroned continued, "Look! I'm making
everything new."

Revelation 21:5

When will things get back to normal?" I asked myself
for the hundredth time. This motherhood thing was wearing me out, even though I was glad to finally be home with
my husband and our new baby.

Bringing Allen home had not been the joyous event I'd
dreamed of during nine months of pregnancy. Nor had it
been the triumphal return I'd hoped for during the seventeen-
day stint in the University of Nebraska's neonatal intensive
care unit (NICU). And the past few days had not been the
cozy scene I'd envisioned during the weeks we spent at my
parents' Iowa home after Allen's release from the hospital.

Instead, I felt like I'd left the restroom and joined the welcome home celebration with toilet paper stuck to my shoe. I was uneasy living seventy miles from the nearest hospital, caring for a baby who, three weeks ago, had been hooked up to tubes and monitors in the NICU. And as a first-time mom, I doubted my ability to distinguish normal baby behaviors from abnormal ones. Memories of our past month's Murphy's Law existence, when everything that could go wrong with our child did, trailed me like toilet paper on a shoe. Worries and doubts clung tenaciously, no matter how hard I tried to shake them.

However, most of the difficulties I experienced when Allen came home stemmed from the changes that accompany the arrival of any new baby rather than from his chronic health condition. But I didn't know that until six years later, after our healthy baby girl was born.

My mother was watching Baby Anne so I could have some alone time with my six-year-old son. We held hands and walked to the library. Well, I walked. He trudged, his bony shoulders slumped. His head drooped as if weighed down by the butch wax that kept his buzz cut standing on end. His usual ear-to-ear grin drooped as well.

"What do you think about being a big brother?" I asked him.

He pushed up his glasses. "Well," he sighed and looked at me, his wide green eyes innocent and trusting, as if he thought I could make the impossible happen. "I just wish things would get back to normal."

I met his gaze and gave him the bad news. "Allen," I said, "things won't ever be like they were before Annie was born. This is the new normal."

He was not amused.

New parents spend nine months dreaming of the day when they will bring their baby home. Parents of sick children dream of the day when their child will leave the hospital. You're dreaming of that day. You're longing for it.

So as you wait, think about the changes that will accompany your child's homecoming. Be realistic about what life at home will be like. And realize that some of the changes you face are ones all parents, not just parents of chronically ill children, have to make.

Allen took about a month to get used to our family's new normal after his sister's arrival rocked his little world. I adjusted to Anne's presence along with him and learned to anticipate rather than resist the changes a new baby brought to my life. "Father," I prayed, "thank you for today's new normal. And prepare me for the new normal I can't yet see."

He's never stopped answering that prayer.

Dear Father, life has been full of changes lately. And as I prepare to take this child home, there are more changes to face. Keep me from attributing all the changes to my child's health condition. Help me to see that some of them are normal and that you are using all of them to make me and our family into something new.

Consider the changes you've experienced since your child became ill. How have they affected you and your family? What changes do you anticipate when your child is dismissed from the hospital?

Take Time to Reflect

32

Pray Big

Be assured that from the day we heard of you,
we haven't stopped praying for you, asking
God to give you wise minds and spirits attuned
to his will, and so acquire a thorough understanding of the ways in which God works.

Colossians 1:9

Bringing a child home from the hospital is supposed to be a joyous event. But if your child is attached to a feeding tube, an IV port, a trach tube, has an immune system so weakened by chemotherapy that you view every visitor as a germ factory, or if your child's diagnosis includes diminished mental ability, the medical paraphernalia and the implications for the future often suffocate your joy. With your child's physical and mental impairments an ever-present reality every moment of the day, paying attention to the spiritual dimensions of that young life is easily overlooked.

To keep spiritual needs front and center, pray for your child's spiritual health whenever you pray for physical health. The content of your prayers, to some degree, depends upon your child's condition. For that reason, Doug and Brenda pray differently for each of their children. Doug prays for the healing of both his children. But because his son, Jeff, has the mental ability of a three or four-year-old, he prays for Jeff to sense God's presence in his life. "To have Jeff at least reach the point where he understands what a prayer is. That he can start a prayer by saying, 'Dear God.'" Jeff now prays daily for God to help his caretakers and family, then ends his prayers with a hearty amen. Beyond that, Doug says, "God has to come in from His perspective and fill him with the rest of it, which I think He's doing. There's no doubt in my mind."

Brenda's prayers for Jeff are similar. "I pray for whatever level he's at, because of the mental retardation, that he will know Jesus." Her prayers for Jessica, who has no mental limitation but whose physical condition causes severe joint pain every day, are different. Now that Jessica's a young adult, Brenda prays for her physical healing and safety, "and of course for her spiritual growth, to be close to the Lord."

One reason Doug is sure God is at work in Jeff's life is he's seen God at work in Jessica's life. "Her faith is probably far more developed than ours is, which is a real blessing.

To be able to keep the mindset that she's keeping, to be able to deal with issues and not let them get her down is just remarkable, and that's got to be a God thing." He describes her attitude before hip surgery her sophomore year of college. "She had a complete peace about God being with her, God being in control of it. I was much, much more apprehensive, and I wasn't even going through the surgery."

Brenda remembers, "Jessica would say, 'However I handle this, I need to do it for the glory of God.' We learned a lot from her."

Doug and Brenda "pray big" for Jeff and Jessica, spiritually, mentally, and physically. They've come to understand that God's love for and intimate knowledge of Jeff is great. The things He is doing within their son are awe-inspiring and praiseworthy, even though they aren't as visible as Jessica's growth and witness.

Your child may be too young to comprehend God with adult maturity. Or your child may never reach that level of comprehension. But even your adult mind can't wholly fathom God's ways. Still, you ask Him to show you more of himself, though you can never fully know Him. The hope that leads you to pray doesn't flow from confidence in your ability. Your hope flows from confidence in a God much bigger than you can comprehend.

Your child's confidence is built upon that same hope. So pray for your child's spiritual health, and expect God to answer in remarkable ways.

Dear Father, help me focus on your love for my child rather than on my child's ability to understand you. So please, Father, let my little one know and love you as completely as possible, not because of who my child is, but because of who you are.

How often do you pray for your child's spiritual health compared to physical well being? How can you pray equally for both? What are your big prayers for your child's relationship with God?

Take Time to Reflect

33

Children Are a Gift from the Lord, Period

Don't you see that children are God's best
    gift?
The fruit of the womb his generous legacy?

Psalm 127:3

From the moment Hiram and I learned of Allen's condition, we knew he had a good chance of living a relatively normal life. And though his first five years were hospital heavy, that prognosis proved true. He did well in school and participated in extra-curricular activities. Now an adult, he's out on his own.

Not every child's future is so rosy. Many parents of kids who survive an initial health crisis know their lives, and their children's lives, will be quite different from what they once expected. If your child is one of those kids, you will grapple with the same issue Bruce and Peggy faced when their second child was a baby.

Their daughter Lacey, born in 1984, has the mental ability of a four or five–month–old infant. Her mental and physical disabilities weren't immediately obvious to her doctor or her parents, though by the time her daughter was three months old, Peggy knew something was wrong.

Throughout the first year of Lacey's life, her limitations became more noticeable. Her parents' lives changed when they decided to keep Lacey in their home as long as they could. They understand that other parents who place severely disabled children in a care facility have made the right choice in their personal situation. "It's not like one's right and one's wrong," Peggy says.

"You have to do what God gives you peace about," Bruce adds. The decision to care for Lacey in their home gave them peace. To accommodate their new lifestyle, Bruce changed employers. "I used to have a job where I traveled and was gone all the time. We knew when Lacey was a year old that I was going to have to be home a lot more."

Early on, many well-meaning people acted like Lacey was a burden her family had to bear, especially for Peggy, whose life revolved around caring for their daughter. Once in a while, Peggy viewed her daughter in the same way. She began to question God. "Children are meant to be a gift from the Lord, not a burden, aren't they? So why is Lacey a burden?"

Deep down, Peggy knew something was wrong with her thinking. One day she sensed God telling her to think about what the Bible says about kids: Children are a gift from the Lord. The light bulb went on, and she understood that the verse wasn't just about the "perfect children," the darling, whole and healthy, look-at-me children. "He doesn't put any clause or condition on this statement. It's just plain, 'Children are a gift from the Lord.'"

In that moment, Peggy realized she'd been asking the wrong question. The question wasn't whether Lacey was a gift or a burden. God said children are always a gift. Instead, He showed her the right questions to ask: How are you going to take care of this gift? How are you going to show the world that Lacey is a gift from the Lord? Those questions changed Peggy's outlook about caring for her daughter. Every day, she tells herself, "I better act like this is a gift." Over the years, she's discovered that when she acts like her daughter is a gift, she thinks of her as a gift.

After more than two decades of caring for her daughter, Peggy wants to pass on this piece of advice to parents of special needs kids: No matter what your child's level of need is—able to lead a normal life, in need of total care, or somewhere in between—you treat your child as a gift, you'll think of your child as a gift. "This child is a gift from the Lord, period," Peggy says. "Start with that foundation and move on from there."

Father, forgive me for viewing my child as a burden. Teach me to act like my child is a gift, even during difficult times, so I will think of this child as a gift. Help those around me see my child is a gift, too.

Do I consider my child a gift from God? Do I treat my child like a gift? How do I show other people that my child is a gift?

Take Time to Reflect

34

Strength, Stamina, Motivation

> "Don't bargain with God. Be direct. Ask for
> what you need."
>
> Matthew 7:7

In the months leading up to Lacey's official diagnosis
as a spastic quadriplegia, Peggy spent a great deal of time
praying for her daughter. When her daughter was between
three and four months old, she says, "I prayed that God
could fix this and no one would know the difference." But
her prayers soon changed. "At four months, I was more like,
'If you're not going to heal her, then I need strength and
peace of mind.'"

Very soon, a deep sense of peace enveloped Peggy. She understood that her prayer had been answered, and God was equipping her to handle her daughter's chronic health condition. That day she began to accept her role as Lacey's caregiver. Before then, she could see what was expected of her, but struggled with it emotionally and mentally. But once she found peace, she thought, "Well, we're moving ahead in the direction of long term."

Peggy's prayers as Lacey's caregiver continued. "Since that day, I've always prayed for God's strength, stamina, and motivation. That is literally my prayer." The need for strength and stamina are obvious, but why does Peggy ask for motivation? Well, she explains, life as a caregiver can be a little redundant. She started doing range of motion exercises when Lacey was two, not realizing she'd still be doing them when Lacey was twenty-four. "Because that seems a little overwhelming, I do pray for motivation to always be at the top of my game for her."

God also provided people to pray for Peggy and Lacey through the Bible study she attended. Though most of the young moms went to evening Bible studies, Peggy chose an afternoon group with older women. They didn't mind if she held Lacey during the meetings until the little girl was old enough to start school.

After a while Peggy realized that she was part of a group of women who were always praying. "That ended up being the hidden blessing of a circle of elderly, widowed women who would say, 'I pray for you and Lacey every day.' Even twenty years later, the ones who are still alive say, 'I just pray for her all the time.'"

When Lacey's condition was diagnosed, Bruce and Peggy had no idea they would be caring for her more than twenty-four years later. "She wasn't supposed to make it to a year," Bruce says.

They have no idea how much longer they will have her. "She does live on the edge," Peggy says, "but she continues to *live* on the edge."

Without prayer, their circumstances would be impossible. Without prayer, your circumstances are impossible, too. But you weren't created to deal with impossible circumstances on your own.

When you pray, you acknowledge your inability to handle things by yourself. That's why Peggy prays for God's strength, stamina, and motivation every day. When you ask people to pray on your behalf and for your child, you admit your need for the support of others. That's why women have been praying for Peggy and Lacey for over twenty years.

Your prayers honor God. Your prayers mean that you trust Him to provide what you can't. So pray often as you care for your child. Pray extravagantly as you pour your energy into your child. Pray confidently, sure that God will answer in unusual and unexpected ways.

Ask others to pray, also. When they ask you what to pray, give them this short and simple list: God's strength, stamina, and motivation. What more do you need?

Dear Father, I can't care for my child's special needs alone. It is not in me to do this. If I am to care for this child, give me enough of your strength to take the first step. Give me stamina to continue. And give me motivation to be the best parent I can be.

When do you most need strength, stamina, and motivation? Who can you ask to be on a prayer team for your family? Who can you ask to share your requests with those on the team?

Take Time to Reflect

35

Thy Will Be Done

> "This is your Father you are dealing with, and
> he knows better than you what you need. With
> a God like this loving you, you can pray very
> simply. Like this:
>> Our Father in heaven,
>> Reveal who you are.
>> Set the world right;
>> Do what's best—as above, so below."
>
> Matthew 6:8–10

Sometimes it is easier to know what *we* need to survive in life—peace, stamina, and motivation—than it is to
discern what our children need. What should we pray for
our kids? For healing? For less pain? For release from the
pain of this world? For a better life to come?

If those questions plague you, you're not alone. Most parents who regularly pray for chronically ill children aren't sure what to request of God. Generally, their prayers progress along a predictable continuum through the years.

When Jason was born and whisked away for surgery, Chuck and Pat prayed the way most traumatized new parents do. "We didn't even care if we had a house; we'd sleep in a tent if He'd just save our little baby." Pat pauses for a moment. Then she and Chuck speak in unison. "You feel like you're making deals."

Reflecting, Pat notes how her prayers have changed through her years as Jason's mom. "Now I would probably pray for whatever's best, whatever God's will is."

Doug and Brenda recognize how their prayers for Jeff and Jessica have changed, too. "Initially, my prayers were almost demanding of God to physically heal both kids and to mentally heal Jeff," says Doug. "As I have grown and matured in my faith, I still have the same prayers that I pray virtually every day, but the prayer has changed now—that if it's God's will, then have Him heal them physically and mentally." Doug adds that he will always pray for healing, "because there's always that possibility."

"But it's *Thy* will be done," Brenda explains. "That's how it's changed."

Naomi, who lost one child and has four others with chronic health issues, faced daily prayer dilemmas. "I didn't know what to pray for them." In the case of her youngest son, the dilemma continues as his needs baffle

158

parents, doctors, and educators. "I still don't know what to pray for Josh." But she knows the attitude she should bring to prayer. "You have to pray where you're at, where your child is. And you have to be real about it. You can't pray, 'Oh, I wish life were back to normal.' You pray based on, 'Okay, whatever life is going to be, that's what I want. God, you take care of it. Help me be ready to accept this. And help my child be prepared for this when it happens.'"

Chuck and Pat's prayers moved from making deals with God to accepting His will. Doug and Brenda's prayers went from a demand for healing to a request for healing, if it was God's will. Naomi's prayers accept the reality of her children's circumstances and ask God to do His will in and through them.

You know where your prayers fall along this continuum. You may not like where you are. You may be impatient to move forward or resent the need to do so. Wherever you are on the continuum, however, one truth will aid your progress: Your prayer attitude is more important than your prayer requests.

Once your prayers spring from a desire to see God's will accomplished in the life of your child, you'll stop wasting energy making deals with God or demanding that He act a certain way. Instead, you'll pray the one prayer God always fulfills: "Our Father in heaven, reveal who you are. Set the world right; do what's best—as above, so below."

Father, I want to pray for your will to be done in my child's life, but what if your will is not what I want? Work within me until I can accept your will for my life and my child's, so I can help my child rest in it, too.

How have you been praying for your child? Where do your prayers fall on the parent/caregiver continuum? How do you want to change the way you pray for your child?

Take Time to Reflect

36

Stay in the Day

> Give your entire attention to what God is
> doing right now, and don't get worked up
> about what may or may not happen tomor-
> row. God will help you deal with whatever hard
> things come up when the time comes.
>
> Matthew 6:34

By nature I'm a planner, an administrator, and a long-range thinker. Planning ahead was as natural to me as breathing, and my abilities served me well as a teacher. They made my life at work and at home easier, and I derived great satisfaction from the efficiency and predictability planning brought to my life.

But those same abilities put me on a collision course with the reality of life as a mother of a totally unpredictable, chronically ill kid. My administrative skills actually hindered my ability to rest in the day or take pleasure in the unexpectedness of now. They certainly didn't teach me to trust God to lead and provide for the tomorrow I couldn't see. So instead of enjoying my son on his good days, I constantly wondered whether my Plan A would be ruined by a sudden illness, and then fussed and fretted over a possible Plan B.

To this day, I'm a better planner than a rester. But over the years I have learned something I wish I'd known when my son was ill, when every single day held an unexpected adventure. As I matured, I learned to make a plan, but then let it go when God's agenda for the day was different from mine.

Peggy implemented the same strategy over twenty years ago. She learned to stick with the biblical principle of not worrying about tomorrow since today has enough trouble of its own. "The pressure of the future and the things that have to be done in two hours or by the end of the week is almost too much with someone like Lacey in your house," Peggy says. Therefore, she trained herself to isolate the hour she was in, the hour when she was holding her daughter or taking her for a walk. She learned to ask herself, "Is there anything so bad in that hour that you can't deal with it?" She discovered there never was. "The more and more you stay in the day, the more and more you realize God works it all out anyway, and you get better at staying in the day."

Peggy explains why staying in the day has been so important. When Lacey was a baby and she worried about what her daughter would be like at age three, anxiety kept her from enjoying Lacey as a baby. If, when Lacey was five, she thought, "What am I going to do if she gets too heavy for me to take care of her?" then those thoughts robbed her of Lacey at five. And if when Lacey was ten, Peggy couldn't enjoy her because she worried about how to deal with her periods when puberty arrived, worry just kept robbing her. "In my case," Peggy says, "it would have robbed me of literally twenty-four years, a quarter of my life, thinking, *What's next?*"

She adds a caution. "It's not that you're in denial, and it's not that you're not planning. I just wouldn't put that thought in charge of your day. That's sort of true even for normal families. If you're always worried about what it's going to be like to have the empty nest, are you enjoying your sixteen-year-old shopping for a prom dress today?"

Peggy's advice is powerful for any parent, but especially for you. With a sick kid in the house, you have to stay in the moment and then strike a healthy balance between that mindset and the need to plan for the future. Otherwise, caring for your child will be overwhelming; the pressure will be too great.

When worry attacks you, practice Peggy's strategy. Isolate the hour you're in, this hour when you are holding your baby or rocking your toddler or rubbing your pre-teen's back and ask yourself, "Is there anything in this hour I can't deal with?" The more you ask the question, the more often you'll receive the answer Peggy has over the last twenty-four years.

Really, there never is.

Father God, when my child's future looks so difficult, it's hard to stay in the moment. But that's what I need to do or I won't enjoy my child's life today. Help me to stay in the day and to entrust the future to you.

What worries are robbing you of joy today? What can you do to isolate the hour and stay in this moment with your child? What joy has your child's life brought to you today?

Take Time to Reflect

37

An Effective Witness

A truthful witness saves lives,
But he who speaks lies is treacherous.
Proverbs 14:25 (NASB)

The day we took our son home, after his three-week stint in NICU, I was scared stiff. "But his breathing is so raspy," I objected.

The nurse patted my arm. "His wheeziness is just due to tracheal malacia. The walls of his bronchial tubes will develop over the next few months, and it will go away."

"He's only been nursing for a week—"

"And he's the unit's star pupil," she countered.

"But we live so far from the hospital."

"You can call us night or day." She tucked a sheet of phone numbers in the diaper bag. "And you have an appointment with the pediatrician in Rapid City on your way home. But your baby's going to be perfectly normal."

At first, her words were true. Allen nursed like a champ and grew rapidly. But after several weeks, he began pulling away from my breast when my let-down reflex triggered and milk flooded into his mouth. His wheezing increased after he nursed. On the Fourth of July, his breathing went from wheeze to rattle, and we were concerned enough to phone the pediatrician at his home on a holiday.

He listened patiently, but was none too pleased. "Your milk comes in too fast. He's a smart baby. He knows it and latches on again once the flood subsides. Don't worry about the wheeziness. It will take months, even years, for that to go away."

His professionalism chastised me. I told myself I was overreacting. What did I know about babies anyway? So I buried my son's alarming symptoms beneath my insecurities as a first-time mom and hung up the phone.

During a midnight feeding three weeks later, Allen pulled away from my breast again. His eyes rolled back in his head. I screamed, "Hiram, he's not breathing! He's not breathing!"

Hiram snatched him and massaged his chest. I called the local EMTs while Allen began gasping for air. A few hours later, the ambulance delivered us to Rapid City Regional Hospital. The next day doctors found that the repair scar in Allen's esophagus had gradually closed. Each time he nursed, less milk trickled through the stricture and more pooled above it. He stopped breathing when the milk overflowed and aspirated into his lungs. Immediately, Allen and I went by Life Flight to the University of Nebraska Hospital in Omaha where doctors performed surgery to insert a feeding tube. Allen received nourishment through the tube for months.

Several surgeries and years of procedures later, he was finally the normal child the NICU nurse had promised.

We could have blamed medical personnel for the complications Allen suffered. But God isn't the God of blame. He's the God of truth. So we took the lessons learned through the experience and used them to help our son battle chronic health problems.

The biggest lesson we learned is the same lesson you will learn as you deal with your child's chronic condition: No one knows the nuances of your child's health like you do. When you think something's wrong, it probably is. And you are your child's best witness. It's up to you to pursue the matter with grace and firmness. It's up to you to describe what you see happening. Speak calmly and knowledgeably. Don't cast blame. Don't be unreasonable. Just tell the truth about what you observe, and don't give up until you get a satisfactory answer.

Once we started to do that, the doctors listened. In fact our pediatrician apologized about the Fourth of July phone call and said, "If I ever have another patient with this condition, I'll refer the parents to you. You're better experts about this than I'll ever be."

The truth is a powerful witness. It saved our child's life. It can save your child's too.

Dear Father, make me an expert about my child's health. Help me be a good observer of the truth and a good communicator with the doctors when I sense something is wrong. Keep me from blaming them when they can't find the answers. Give me strength to speak the truth until they do.

What concerns do you have about your child's chronic health condition? How does your doctor respond when you communicate your concerns? If you feel you're being ignored, what can you do to communicate more effectively?

Take Time to Reflect

38

Nothing's Gonna Stop Us Now

Are you hurting? Pray.
Do you feel great? Sing.

James 5:13

Kids love music, and kids love fun. That's why the creators of *Howdy Doody, Captain Kangaroo, Sesame Street, Barney, Mr. Rogers,* and every other successful kids' TV series have made music an integral element of their shows. Because kids think music is synonymous with fun.

If you're sitting at home with a sick, fussy kid, and the doctors have told you that your child will be sick and fussy for an extended period of time, perhaps forever, you are not thinking about singing. You are not thinking about having fun. Or dancing. Or playing. Or any of the things that tickle a kid's fancy. You are thinking about how to survive the day.

You need to remember a little secret that children are born knowing: one of the best ways to survive the day is with music and a little fun. That's why Jenny and her mom claimed a favorite song during her years of chemo treatment.

The pop song "Nothing's Gonna Stop Us Now," recorded by Starship, hit the charts in 1987, shortly after Jenny's cancer was diagnosed. "Whenever we were having a bummer day or I was feeling sick, we would do something fun. Like put on the song, or we would make M & M cookies. I would sort all the colors of M & Ms, and then we would do something fun."

Notice how a little music segued straight into fun for Jenny? I saw it happen as a teacher, too. The most painful subject matter—multiplication, earth science, geography—became the kids' favorites when the information was set to music, the cornier the better.

The same thing can happen at your house when you turn on the CD player. If you add a little creativity and get goofy with your child, your family might do more than survive the day; they might enjoy it, too.

The hard days with our sick son, who in addition to his esophageal complications seemed to pick up every bacterial and viral infection possible during his first five years of life, softened a bit with music. When we rocked, I put his name in place of Conrad Birdie's in the farewell song from the musical *Bye, Bye, Birdie*. The tension drained from both of us as I sang, and he hummed along. When he got older, we didn't wait until December to play the John Denver and the Muppets Christmas album. We calypso danced around the house to the Latin version of Miss Piggy warbling, "Christmas is coming, the goose is getting fat," laughing until our sides ached, even on the hottest summer days.

Music can make your hard days easier, too. Choose a song or make one up with your child and make it your family anthem. When the day turns blue, turn on the music and make the day fun. Hold your youngster in your arms and dance. Sit in the rocking chair and sing to your baby. Turn on the CD player, sort M & Ms, and make cookies.

Every kid likes to have fun, even one with a chronic illness. Parents, even those with sick kids, should have fun with their children. Because God made kids to have fun.

Jenny experienced the power of music during illness, and she wants your child to experience it, too. "It's easy to get caught up in everyday happenings, but each day is a blessing." She urges parents to spend time with their kids and do something special with them. "Do something like listen to a song or make cookies or whatever it is to let their kids know they are happy they're here, that they're alive."

Dear Father, I am so glad for this day with my child. Thank you for making my child love music and fun. Show me how to enjoy music with my child, and give me a childlike spirit of fun. Help us laugh and enjoy life together today.

What songs does my child enjoy? How can I change the words of a song to make it our song? When can I inject a little music into our days?

Take Time to Reflect

One Step Ahead
All the Way

God went ahead of them in a Pillar of Cloud
during the day to guide them on the way, and
at night in a Pillar of Fire to give them light ...
The Pillar of Cloud by day and the Pillar of Fire
by night never left the people.

Exodus 13:21–22

Parents of chronically ill children need extra physical, spiritual, and emotional support. Bruce and Peggy credit church friends, the schools, adult day-care facilities, and the Department of Human Services for providing services and encouragement that have enhanced their ability to care for Lacey and improved the quality of her life.

But in Bruce's eyes, their greatest support comes from God, who works through those agencies and people to provide for his daughter. "He's been one step ahead for her provision all the way through."

"That's been kind of fun in a sense," Peggy agrees. When they first moved to the town where they now live, Lacey was a baby. At that time their school district bused students with severe and profound special needs to participate in a neighboring town's program. Because Lacey choked frequently, Peggy wasn't eager to have her on a bus twice a day. Still, she didn't pray for God to change the arrangement. "I tend to go with the rule rather than think something different could be prayed about for school. So that was something I never thought to pray about."

But the summer before Lacey started school, the neighboring district's special classroom for children with severe and profound needs was full. At the same time, the population of special needs children in the local community increased. The district decided to open a new program in the fall. The program provided stimulation and therapy for Lacey, and her absence during the day gave Peggy a needed break. To top it off, the classroom was in the elementary building closest to their home. Peggy smiles. "It was right out my back door."

Throughout Lacey's school career, when she went from elementary to middle school and then from middle school to high school, the scenario repeated itself. At each juncture the district opened a new program, perfectly tailored to meet Lacey's needs, where none had existed before.

But the community didn't have an adult day-care facility suitable for Lacey when she turned twenty-one and graduated from the public school system, so the year before her milestone birthday, Bruce and Peggy prepared to shoulder the bulk of their daughter's care. Then, during that year, a senior citizen day-care facility opened in town. "I had no idea that was even in the works," Peggy says. She approached the director about Lacey. They didn't know there was a need for people in her age group. "But they weren't full," Peggy explains. "They needed more clientele so that was perfect for Lacey."

Even when they didn't know what they needed, when they didn't know how to pray, God walked ahead of Lacey and her parents every step of the way. He provided beyond what they expected or imagined. Today, because of His past leading, they trust Him to provide for Lacey's future.

When God's provision for your child doesn't seem to match what is needed, when every available solution is inadequate, when you don't have a clue of how to ask, you will be hard-pressed to trust God to provide. When you reach that point, take a few moments to review past unexpected provisions: the friend who gave exactly the right gift, the advice that led to a solution you didn't know existed, the surprising answer to a question you didn't know to ask.

Those happenings are God's footprints. Find the footprints and you'll find God in the place He always promises to be: a step ahead of you all the way.

Father, I am inadequate to meet my child's needs. I don't know what's available. I don't know what we need. I don't know what to ask for. All I have to hang onto is your promise to walk ahead of us. Please, Father, provide for us and give me faith to trust your provision.

How have you seen God provide for your child's needs in unexpected ways? When has His provision been less dramatic but still obvious? When is it difficult to trust His provision?

Take Time to Reflect

The Death of Dreams

Losing a Child

40

The Death of Dreams

There is no room in love for fear. Well-formed love banishes fear.

1 John 4:18

I threw the glass as hard as I could. Though it was made of indestructible plastic, guaranteed not to break, it shattered against the kitchen wall along with my dreams for a healthy baby. Allen had endured eight months of surgeries. The follow-up procedures that dilated his esophagus made him so skittish, he refused to open his mouth when we offered him spoonfuls of baby food. We hadn't found a formula he could tolerate, so I was still pumping breast milk, but never enough to satisfy his hunger. My inadequate efforts to feed him fed my fears as well.

I leaned against the kitchen counter, sobbing. A hand touched my shoulder, and a voice whispered in my mind, "What are you afraid of, Jolene?" I looked and saw no one. The voice continued. "What's the worst that could happen?"

I turned to face my deepest fear. "My baby could die."

"Why are you afraid if that's the worst that could happen?"

I stood, grabbed a broom, and began sweeping up the plastic shards that littered the floor. I didn't want to name my fear, but the voice within forced me to confront it.

"Do you believe I am a loving God?"

"Yes, Lord."

"Why?"

"Because you gave everything to save your children. You sacrificed your Son to show the depths of your love and to save us."

"So, Jolene, if you truly believe that, what is the worst thing that could happen?"

I stopped sweeping. "My dreams for Allen would die."

"And what is your most cherished dream, Jolene?"

"That he will know your love and spend eternity with you." As the implications of those words sunk in, my knees gave way. I sat on the floor, sure that the loving God who sacrificed His Son loved my son, too. If Allen died, this loving God would take my son, too young to choose or reject God for himself, to live in the presence of His love forever.

For the first time, I understood that the death I feared could be the realization of my ultimate dream for Allen. I grieved at the thought of his death—how it would end our relationship with our baby boy and snatch away the joy of watching him grow. And yet I also rejoiced to think that his death could be an outpouring of grace, the fulfillment of a cherished dream which, if Allen lived, he might one day choose to reject for eternity.

If your child is close to death, you need to confront your fears. Otherwise, something inside you will break. For fear shatters everything you think is indestructible—your relationships, your dreams, your hope, your faith—unless you overcome it.

If the fear of death stalks you today, confront it by considering the love of God. Consider the Father who loved us so much He sent His Son to die for us. Consider the Son who humbled himself, who came to earth to live as a man so He could demonstrate the depths of His love through His death on a cross. Consider that love, strong and deep enough to cast out fear.

Sitting on our kitchen floor surrounded by shards of broken plastic and the love of God, my fear disappeared. Soon Hiram noticed a difference. I was calmer, he said, better able to handle Allen's continuing trials.

The change in me was a good thing. Because when Allen hit puberty, complete with pimples, poor choices, and numerous trials, my relationship with him nearly shattered. The only thing that saved it was my faith in the God whose perfect love, indestructible and guaranteed not to break, held us safe in His firm and gentle hands.

Father of life, I don't want my child to die. I want to see the dreams I have for my child come to pass. I am so afraid. So Father, I am asking you to show me your perfect love that casts out fear. Help me get rid of the fear by trusting your love for me and my child.

What dreams do you have for your child? What fears threaten those dreams? How can understanding Christ's love help you deal with your fears?

Take Time to Reflect

41

When to Let Go

> There's an opportune time to do things, a right
> time for everything on the earth:
> A right time for birth and another for death ...
> Ecclesiastes 3:1–2

Although Allen nearly died as an infant, he lived and is still part of our lives. But not every family's story has this kind of ending. Often parents have to make decisions about further treatment that affect the remainder of a child's life while reeling from the shock of a terminal prognosis. How can they make wise and loving, ethical decisions as they anticipate the deepest sorrow a parent can know—the death of a precious child?

Jeff and Carolyn made decisions like that after their daughter's cancer returned. Beth, then two, was hospitalized for the last month of her life. Carolyn remembers their struggle during those final weeks: "When do you stop praying for healing and decide to let her go? Let her have the process happen?" Carolyn doesn't recall discussing the decision. She doesn't even remember how or when they made the decision; just that it seemed somewhat clear at the time. "And I can remember feeling a lot of guilt from other people because they didn't understand how we could love her and ever let a child die."

But Jeff and Carolyn loved their daughter so much that they based their decisions on her needs rather than their own. Of course they wanted their child to live; but when that wasn't possible, they wanted her death to be free of pain and fear. Carolyn describes the last month of Beth's life: "It took about a month as far as she was no longer living, but in the process of dying. I think they asked us, 'Do you want to use stronger drugs?'" They told the doctors to give medication that would slow the growth of the cancer cells so Beth wouldn't have pain in her legs, but not so harsh as to make her sick.

Beth died in early September of 1982 at the age of two years and two months. Carolyn's voice wavers, and she cries for a moment as she talks about that day. "Beth didn't ever seem fearful of anything … she certainly had *His* loving arms. She had ours, too."

Carolyn was surprised by some of her emotions the day Beth died. "I remember the relief. There was also a little guilt, because we didn't have to worry about her anymore.

I felt like she was tucked away in a spot, like putting your child to bed when they're little. It was a comfortable and trusting thing."

Dr. Jones, a pediatrician and a mom, came to accept death as part of life while working with children at her church. When the kids in her catechism class were writing get well cards to ill parish members, though she knew some of them wouldn't recover, her perspective about death changed. "Death is a cycle of life," she realized. And her new perspective led to a new question: "How do you pray, not for the obvious, but to incorporate this episode into your life and be able to live with it and move on and realize that things do continue?"

If your child's condition is terminal, Dr. Jones's questions have meaning for you. How do you accept death as part of life? How can you live with the loss and the grief and eventually move on? If your doctor or nurses haven't put you in contact with hospice workers yet, ask them to do so. They help patients and families deal with those questions and support them when it's time to let go.

Involve others as you make hard decisions and face great loss. And let Carolyn's words, birthed in grief and pain and hope, reassure you. "The stability of family, the stability of faith, and the stability of friends will get people through." Then she adds, very quietly, "Sometimes we forget there's something beyond this everyday life."

Dear Father who loves my child, my heart is breaking at the thought of life without my little one. How can we decide to let this precious child go? Help us make decisions based on what's best for our child rather than what we want. Give us faith to trust in the life beyond this everyday existence.

If you are facing your child's death, who can answer your medical and ethical questions? Who will support you as you make decisions about the end of your child's life? Who can you ask to contact hospice for you?

Take Time to Reflect

42

Dancing with Two Left Feet

Are there no healing ointments in Gilead?
Isn't there a doctor in the house?
So why can't something be done to heal and
save my dear, dear people?

Jeremiah 8:22

A hush fell over the delivery room when Scott and Penni's son was born. Something was wrong. Later, they would learn that Evan had Noonan syndrome, a genetic birth disorder which includes heart abnormalities, but at that moment all Scott knew was that something was wrong with their new baby. In a panic, he asked the doctor, "Is he going to die? Is he going to die?"

"Scott," the doctor replied, "we all die."

Some people might have interpreted the doctor's words as harsh and uncaring, but Scott didn't. The words reminded him of what we know but try to ignore: We all die. Death is part of life.

Pediatric physicians—the oncologists, surgeons, gastro-intestinal doctors, and cardiologists—who treat serious childhood illnesses will never save all their patients. When a child's health fails, the only thing doctors can do is walk with the parents on the pathway to death.

Dr. Ashcraft, a pediatric surgeon, says that during the final days and hours of a child's life, doctors have to muster as much compassion as they can and still maintain enough objectivity to get through the day. "You can't let yourself get terribly, terribly involved with a child or it just hamstrings you. For instance, if you do one very difficult heart surgery in the morning and the patient dies, you have to go out and comfort the parents … and then go smiling into the next room and tell the parents of the next heart patient that everything is probably going to be okay. That is difficult."

Dr. Hopkins, another pediatric surgeon, suppresses the emotional aspects of some cases. "But I am not hesitant to ask the chaplains for help. I never feel that I can ever give parents very good advice." A pediatric oncologist, Dr. Jones says that in some cases when she has had to share the news with the parents that their child has died unexpectedly, she wishes she could do it over again. "I felt I came across as—professional is not the word, experienced is not the word, and compassionate is not the word because I think I have all of those. But I felt like I was dancing with two left feet."

All three doctors maintain outward professionalism when faced with a child's death, but inside they dance with two left feet. And they execute their dances in their own unique ways.

Dr. Ashcraft has become friends of the families of some patients who were chronically ill and had many operations. "You develop a real rapport or friendship with the parents. I've gone to funerals. I've been a pallbearer at some of my patients' funerals. It's difficult."

Dr. Hopkins always tries to maintain a presence with his patients' families. "You want people to realize you have some caring for them. Sharing similar experiences with them probably is the most single valuable thing to do. So they don't think it's the only time it's ever happened."

Dr. Jones uses her past experience to help her better serve her present patients. Even so, she often thinks about the children she has cared for, the ones who didn't survive, and asks herself, "How old would they be now? How have the families done?"

So if your doctor remained professional and objective when your child died, realize it was not because he didn't care, but because that's what doctors have to do—dance with two left feet. It's part of the job.

Father, thank you for the doctors who tried to save my child's life. Be with the doctors and nurses as they grieve. Help all of us heal as we face the hard truth that death is part of life.

How did your doctor show compassion toward your child and your family? How do you think the doctor is grieving for your child? What can you do to express your gratitude for the doctor's efforts?

Take Time to Reflect

43

The Black Hole
of Depression

The enemy ... put me in a black hole,
buried me like a corpse in that dungeon.
I sat there in despair, my spirit draining away,
my heart heavy like lead.

Psalm 143:3

Lyn and Sherri were shocked by the death of their first child. One day they were first time, expectant parents. The next day, they were grieving for their dead newborn daughter. People in their small town rallied around them. The elderly pastor wrote a poem in memory of little Sherri Lyn. The owner of the furniture store where they had picked out a crib canceled the order without being asked. People sent cards. Women who were mere acquaintances wrote beautiful letters about children they had lost.

Lyn's work helped him move forward. "I had a job and coaching to go to," he explains. "I didn't sit home and think about all these things like Sherri had to."

Sherri had resigned from her teaching post the previous spring to stay home as a full-time mom. But instead of caring for a baby, she planned a funeral, and the October days that followed were long and unbearable. She sank into a deep depression. "I would get Lyn off to school, and then I would crawl into bed and sort of burrow in. Then I would make myself get up and be ready to greet him when he came home."

She made a scrapbook of the cards and letters to take to her parents' home at Christmas and share with her relatives, but her effort fizzled. "I had aunts who didn't know we'd lost a baby. They didn't talk about it. So it wasn't fun that first year."

Sherri's depression continued after the Christmas holidays. She desperately wanted to get pregnant again, but it didn't happen, and she grew more depressed. "I'd sleep until noon. I didn't have anything else to do."

Two women reached in to lift her out of her black hole. The first was a former teaching colleague, Rosie. She and her husband, Hoag, had become second parents to the grieving couple. When she saw what was happening to Sherri, Rosie asked her to clean for her. Sherri smiles. "She knew I needed to get out of the house." Shortly after that, a special education job opened up in the rural school where

Rosie taught, and Sherri applied and was hired. "So she and I took turns driving." As they drove to work and back, they talked.

The second woman to help was Sherri's college roommate, Joy. Her first child had died of the same malady as Lyn and Sherri's daughter, at almost the same time. When they talked on the phone, Joy said, "I've just got to believe God's going to make me stronger through this."

"Just believe," Sherri says. "That kind of stuck."

Slowly, her depression lifted. She couldn't pinpoint how or when she came out of her black hole. "It just kind of faded" is her best explanation.

Sherri's battle may sound familiar to you. You may be fighting depression today, floundering in a black hole, your spirit draining away, your heart heavy as lead. Your feelings are normal, nearly universal for parents who love their children and lose them.

But if such crushing grief becomes the entire focus of your being, depression will overwhelm you. It will lock you in the dungeon of your despair. The only way to keep that from happening is to grab hold of the hands that reach out to you. When a Rosie appears in your life and offers you a cleaning job, accept it. When the opportunity arises to do meaningful work for others, take it. When the Joy from your past shares the story of her grief with you, listen and share your story, too.

Slowly, though you may never pinpoint exactly how or when it happened, your depression will fade. You'll be stronger. You'll be ready to live again.

Dear Father, I have never known grief like this before. I miss my child so much. All I can think about is my loss and the emptiness inside me. Give me something else to think about so I can heal. Send people who understand my grief and will talk to me. Lead me out of this dungeon of despair.

Are you exhibiting any of these signs of depression? Are you sleeping much of the day? Are your thoughts constantly consumed by your loss? Do you feel hopeless? If you suspect you are depressed, call your doctor, pastor, or a mental health counselor and ask for help.

Take Time to Reflect

44

Grief Is a Team Sport

So speak encouraging words to one another.
Build up hope so you'll all be together in this,
no one left out, no one left behind. I know
you're already doing this; just keep on doing it.

1 Thessalonians 5:11

Grief is a team sport. Players are drafted onto the team, not because they're winners, but because they've lost so much. The goal of the game varies from day to day. Sometimes the goal is to get out of bed in the morning. Sometimes the goal is to put one foot ahead of the other throughout the day. Sometimes the goal is to breathe, to eat, to feel, to hope. But the players can't meet their goals alone. Because grief's a team sport, and team members only win by sticking together.

When Naomi's oldest son, Joel, died of brain cancer at age three, one of the most valuable players on her team was her friend DeAnn. Naomi calls their relationship a gift from God. The two women had been friends for fourteen years when their sons were born two days apart and died of the same cancer four weeks apart. "So we went through it together and grieved together and knew exactly how the other felt at all times. We are able to go through our cycles of grief together. We understand how the other thinks, so we have each other always, under any circumstance. And that's an incredible gift."

To find someone with a grief as identical as Naomi and DeAnn's is rare. To find other parents who can share your grief is not. When Twyla's second child was stillborn, she was contacted by another woman in town who had also lost a baby. The woman invited Twyla to a Compassionate Friends meeting, and Twyla attended a few meetings with her new friend. "It was very helpful because you hear everybody's story and you see that you're not alone. There are always stories that are worse than yours. You get empathy for other people."

Chuck and Pat's second son, Christopher, died at birth because a bronchial genic cyst blocked his airway. They attended Compassionate Friends, too. The organization provided the support Chuck needed, but Pat says she needed more because she hadn't handled the trauma very well. "I didn't like making people uncomfortable, and so I would act like nothing was wrong. After Christopher,

I ended up going to a counselor and I was just a mess. 'Cause I'd never gone through the grieving." The counselor introduced her to another woman who had lost a child. When the woman joined Pat's team, she started to heal.

We were created to rejoice and grieve together, to share in one another's lives and support each other. God brought DeAnn and Naomi together. He brought a new friend to Twyla. He used a counselor to connect Pat with another grieving woman. These teams weren't accidental. They were orchestrated by God to help those parents heal.

If you have lost a child or are facing such a loss, you need to let people join your team. Don't huddle alone on the sidelines, wrapped in a blanket of grief, isolated by the pain of your injuries. The only way to get from where you are today to where you need to be one day in the future is to become a team player, to let other parents who have lost children into your life.

Like you, they've lost much. Like you, they grieve every day. They are the ones who can help you to breathe again, eat again, hope again. They are an incredible gift from God. Let them be part of your team.

Dear Father, I come to you with my grief because you know what it's like to lose a child. You know how much I need to talk to another parent who has lost a child. Bring someone to be part of my team so I don't have to grieve alone.

Has your child's doctor put you in contact with any support groups? Who can help you locate a grief counselor of the closest chapter of Compassionate Friends? The hospital chaplain or social worker? Your church pastor? Good friends? Family members?

Take Time to Reflect

45

The Power of a Name

Can a mother forget the infant at her breast,
   walk away from the baby she bore?
But even if mothers forget,
   I'd never forget you—never.
Look, I've written your names on the backs of
   my hands.

Isaiah 49:15–16

Shawn entered first grade the fall after Allen was born. He was one of my country school students for the next three years until we moved to a different state. When news came nearly two decades later that Shawn, by then a young husband and father, had died, we were stunned. Within a few months we drove to South Dakota to grieve with Gerald and Becky, Shawn's parents.

"Come with us to the cemetery," Becky said when we arrived. So we gathered around Shawn's grave, his parents, my husband and I, on a sunny August day. As we examined the headstone, I wanted to talk about everything except Shawn. Surely, I reasoned, talking about their son and saying his name over and over would pick at the new scabs on their hearts and cause them to bleed again. But standing on the windswept hill in the prairie, not far from the place where I had taught Shawn to read and memorize his multiplication tables, I couldn't stay silent. I told his parents every story I could recall about their beloved son, stopping often to laugh and cry and wipe away my tears.

Gerald, a soft-spoken and burly rancher, looked at the ground, then up at me. "Thanks for saying his name, Jolene." His eyes were bright with tears. "So many people are afraid to say Shawn's name."

People are often reluctant to say a deceased child's name, especially to the parents who chose the name. Such sensitivity is well-meant but misguided. Parents want to hear their deceased child's name spoken. Gerald and Becky did. So did Wayne and Sandy.

When Sandy was four months pregnant, she and Wayne learned their baby was anacephalic, without a brain, and would die at birth. Soon afterward, they named their baby Ethan. "We'd picked out some names, but at four months in the pregnancy you don't address the child by name," Wayne explains. "But someone suggested, 'Go ahead and call him by name. That makes it more personal and more a part of us.'"

Even now, many years later, Sandy often thinks of Ethan. "He would have been fourteen in August. And he'd probably be playing baseball and basketball. What color would his hair be? Would he have been tall? Would he have looked like Wayne? Would he have had glasses?" Always as she thinks of him and when she talks about him, she calls him by name.

Jeff, who lost his daughter Beth to cancer, shares grief counseling strategies with teachers in a class he frequently facilitates. He tells them to use the name of the deceased when speaking to family members. When his students lose family members, usually grandparents, he goes to the visitation and finds the kids and sits down beside them. "Tell me a funny story about you and your grandpa." And he calls everyone, the survivors and the deceased, by name.

A spoken name evokes great power. The choice of your child's name was deliberate and meaningful to you. You devoted much time and thought to the decision and then packed the name full of a lifetime of hopes and dreams. When your child's life ended, the name remained. Each time it's spoken, the preciousness of your child's life is confirmed, made real, acknowledged.

God knows how much you want to hear your child's name. And He heals you, bit by tiny bit, each time someone uses it in your presence. After all, God has your child's name written on the back of His hand. He promises it will never be forgotten.

Dear Father, I see people hesitate and avoid saying my child's name. Give me words to tell them how much I want to hear it spoken, to convey the comfort hearing the name brings. Thank you for the gift of names.

Why is it hard for people to use your child's name when speaking to you? What can you say or do to dispel that fear? How has using your child's name helped you grieve?

Take Time to Reflect

46

Let Grief Embrace You

You're blessed when you feel you've lost what
is most dear to you. Only then can you be
embraced by the One most dear to you.

Matthew 5:4

I felt strangely detached from what was happening the
night Allen quit breathing as I nursed him, more like a spectator watching a movie than like the parent of a child fighting for his life. The same sense of detachment surrounded
me whenever Allen faced a health crisis: when we climbed
into an ambulance, boarded the Life Flight airplane, or
when nurses wheeled him to surgery on a stretcher.

After each crisis passed—sometimes within hours,
sometimes a few days later, sometimes the next month—the
reality of the experience crashed down upon me: *My baby*

nearly died in my arms. The top surgeon in the country said he'd never seen a case like Allen's before. The doctors can't do anything more. My child may not live. And after each traumatic event, when my mind and body were strong enough to face the pain, I would grieve. I would ask God hard questions about my son's suffering and slowly work through the answers.

For parents who lose a child, the grieving process takes not just weeks and months, but years. For Jeff and Carolyn, the ritual of the visitation and the funeral carried them through the days right after Beth's death. But later on, Jeff says, "There were times of not feeling clear. It was kind of hard to go to church right away, too. In fact, there's sort of an irony in that. Your faith should be your biggest support. But it's also your anger and confusion."

Carolyn says many people told her to give herself a year to recover. "I can remember getting to the end of one year and saying, 'What's this? I don't feel any different.'" But, she says, somewhere between two and five years, the physical ache stopped. "That's not really encouraging when you think, 'We'll be doing five years of grieving?' That seems like a really long time."

Two to five years is a long time. But Jeff says it's important not to rush the process. "The grief process takes a lot of time. You have to allow it—instead of going after it—to let it wrap itself around you. Faith is a great comfort after you get over the anger. No matter how spiritual you are, you're going to have those questioning moments. 'What in the world? What kind of God would do this?'"

Finding answers to those questions takes a long time, but Jeff advises, "Be patient and let healing come to you instead of trying to go after it." As he and Carolyn healed, they found great joy in their memories of their daughter. "Beth did so many funny things in her short little life, and we think about some of the funny things. It's amazing what a little laughter can do."

Once Carolyn worked through her grief, her belief in the goodness and purpose of Beth's life grew. Her middle school students often ask her, "Would you rather Beth hadn't been born?" And though her daughter's life was full of hospital stays and chemo treatments and loss, Carolyn's answer is emphatic. "Even though she went through things, I would have wanted her. I learned so much."

If the loss of your child is recent, your grief is still an open wound. The healing Jeff and Carolyn have experienced seems unattainable to you, a cruel and futile hope. You can't imagine ever reaching their level of acceptance or finding any comfort in the God who took your child. Your anger with Him is palpable and painful. Your lack of faith is frightening.

The grieving process will take a long time. You can't chase after it. You can't force it, only wait for it. Allow it to wrap itself around you. And one day, though you can't imagine it now, the physical ache will stop. You'll think of the funny things your child once did, and you'll laugh. You'll begin to heal.

Father of all sorrow, my grief is so deep. How can a wound like this ever heal? How will I ever live with such loss? Please, Father, wrap your arms around me so I can bear this painful reality and wait for healing to come.

How can you allow the grief process to come to you instead of chasing after it? How has the loss of your child made you question God?

Take Time to Reflect

47

Comfortless Platitudes

If God didn't hesitate to put everything on
the line for us, embracing our condition and
exposing himself to the worst by sending his
own Son, is there anything else he wouldn't
gladly and freely do for us?

Romans 8:32

Somewhere along your grief journey you will need to resist the urge to cram comfortless platitudes spoken by well-intentioned but thoughtless people back down their throats. Parents who outlive their children have their own "top ten list" of things not to say when a child dies. The one platitude that shows up most often on the list: "I know what you're going through. I know how you feel."

You'll have to bite your tongue and swallow hard when you hear that one. And file it for future reference, because from now on you will know, like Jeff does, what not to say when tragedy strikes another family. "I never say, 'Call me if you need anything,' because they never call. I just go and mow somebody's lawn or shovel somebody's sidewalk because that's what was done for me. I never say, 'I know how you feel,' because nobody knows how I felt, and I don't know how you feel."

Chuck echoes Jeff's words, but adds a caveat. "A lot of people say that kind of thing, but it's empty. You need somebody who's lost a child who can truly say, 'I know just what you're experiencing.'" People think they can imagine what it's like. "You really can't," Chuck says, his voice low and sad, "unless you've been there."

Because my son survived his childhood illness, I don't know how you feel. But I do know what it's like to have someone truly understand a deep and lasting sorrow.

As a young adult, our son went through a long period of rebellion, and at its height, he rejected our lifestyle, our values, and my love with a cruelty that left me utterly bereft. A few months later three young men from our town, all a year or two younger than Allen, died in a terrible car accident. My heart was heavy on the day I went to visit Denise, the mother of Joe, one of the young men. The pain of my son's rejection was raw and constant, and I couldn't help comparing the loss of our relationship to Denise's much greater, final loss. I pulled into her driveway and scolded myself for comparing my pain to hers.

Her grief was evident, written on her face, pressing on her shoulders, weighing down her hands when she met me at the door. But she welcomed my company, and our conversation grew easier the longer I stayed. We talked about our daughters who were in the same high school class, about her son Joe, and then she asked about my son. Briefly, I told her about his recent decision.

Then Denise, whose loss and suffering outstripped anything I have known, offered comfort so deep that the memory of her words still brings me to tears. "Then you know how I feel," she said. "You know what it's like to lose the dreams you had for your son, too."

The kindness of her words stunned me. Out of her deep ocean of grief, she validated my cupful of suffering. And with her words I began to recover from my son's rejection. For many months they comforted me because they were not cheap platitudes. They were truth, born of her lost dreams and our shared sorrow.

I can't return Denise's kindness because I don't know how she feels. All I can do is pray for her and ask the God who lost His Son on the cross two thousand years ago to comfort her. He alone can comfort the grief she bears for Joe. So I pray for her and trust God to ease her sorrow, to comfort her raw and aching heart because He knows exactly how she feels.

Dear Father, did your heart break when your Son died? Did you cry when He breathed His last breath? If you understand my grief, please help me. I need someone who knows exactly how I feel to cry with me and share my tears.

Which cheap platitudes do you hope you never hear again? What words of comfort have you heard? Who has comforted you in profound and lasting ways?

Take Time to Reflect

48

The Ones Who Cried

You've kept track of my every toss and turn
through the sleepless nights,
Each tear written in your ledger,
each ache written in your book.

Psalm 56:8

When a child dies, the loss reaches beyond the family circle. Though the grief of those on the perimeter of your child's life may not be as deep or profound as yours, their mourning is real. As those people work through their feelings, they will share with you in many ways, some predictable, some surprising, and some wholly unexpected. Amazingly, much of your healing will begin as people grieve with you and as you witness the impact of your child's life on others.

Jeff's middle school students were a great source of comfort to him when his two-year-old daughter, Beth, died early in the school year. Many students attended the funeral and wrote cards. They continued to offer their condolences when he returned to school, and he could tell that parents and the substitute teacher had coached them about what to say. Their thoughtfulness eased his reentry into the classroom. But for students unacquainted with illness and death, his return was still an awkward time.

One student, Adam, however, provided a moment of exceptional healing. Adam was one of Beth's favorite babysitters. His father had a chronic health condition, so the boy was sensitive to long-term illnesses. When Jeff drove the forty-five miles to Beth's chemo treatments, Adam rode in the backseat and played with the toddler. But at the hospital when the chemo was administered, he sat in the waiting room. Once Jeff jokingly asked him if he'd like to go in to observe the treatment. "No," Adam told him. "I'll just be here when she comes out. She'll come right to me, I know."

Beth's struggle with cancer affected Adam deeply, and after she died, he was sad for a long time. "He was probably the hardest hit of all my students," Jeff said.

Many students were excused from school to attend Beth's funeral. Adam was among them. Later that evening, Jeff received a phone call from him. "I was at the funeral, but you didn't notice me," Adam said. "You were kind of a wreck, so I made a list of all the students who came to the funeral. And I put little stars by the ones who cried."

Adam and his classmates grieved with the sweet awkwardness and transparency of children. Most adults won't be so transparent. Their expressions will be colored by age, their familiarity with illness and death, and by their relationship with your child and your family.

Some people will give money to honor your child's memory. Some will bring food to nourish your bodies. Others will offer to mow your lawn or shovel your snow while you tend to pressing business. Someone may send stamps to use on your thank you notes. Someone may loan dress clothes for your family members to wear to the funeral. The offerings will be as varied as the people who present them, but their intent will be the same. They want you to see that your child's life touched them and that your loss makes them sad.

Their outpourings of love will turn your attention beyond your personal grief to the people touched by your child's life and your family's struggle. Their expressions of sympathy, in various forms, will bring comfort and healing, and your responses to them, even the physical act of writing thank you notes, will provide tangible proof of the existence and importance of your child's short life. God moves people to demonstrate how your child impacted their lives. It's one of His ways of showing you how valuable your child's life is to Him. With each heartfelt expression of grief, God says, "The names of all those mourning over your loss are written in my ledger." Just like Adam, He wants you to know, "These are the ones who cried."

Father God, thank you for showing me how much my child's life matters to others. Thank you for the expressions of sympathy from so many people. Use their concern and care to heal the deep pain of loss in all of us.

How has God used the grief of others to help you heal? What expressions of sympathy have been especially meaningful to you and your family? What proof do you have that your child's life had value and impacted the lives of others?

Take Time to Reflect

49

They Are Changed People

> Become the kind of container God can use to
> present any and every kind of gift to his guests
> for their blessing.
>
> 2 Timothy 2:21

When a child is born, parents welcome a new life into their world. When a serious illness affects that child, their world is shaken. When their child dies, the world shatters and leaves a litter of lost hopes and heartbreak, abandoned dreams and empty arms, anger and grief.

In the midst of such devastation, parents don't live; they only exist. To live again, they have to pick their way through the fragments of their old world, salvage what they can, and find a reason to move forward. Making their way through the brokenness takes a long, long time. When they finally get past the devastation, the majority find the experience has changed them in meaningful ways.

The first change was immediate for Lyn and Sherri. Their infant daughter's death confirmed their decision for Sherri to stay home with their kids. Lyn says there were other changes over the years, especially when other crises arose. "Something happens, it's not the end of the world. It's not that dramatic compared to the loss of a child."

"We appreciate day-to-day," Sherri adds. "I think through the whole thing it made our marriage very strong because we had to depend on each other." The changes reach beyond their family relationships. Sherri is committed to showing new parents how much their babies are loved. She spearheads a "letter nursery" at her church. "When a new baby is born at church, I write them a little note every three months until they're three years old."

Beth's death changed Jeff and Carolyn, too. "As a family it made us cherish and value the time we have. Carolyn not returning to work until our kids were older . . . that was huge," Jeff says. And it affected the way he does his job. "I had this big change in the way I treated kids. I think this helped mold me into the teacher I am today. Also, I'm more aware of what to say and not to say, what to do and not to do in tragedies and deaths."

When her children were older, Carolyn became a family and consumer science teacher. She uses her experience when she teaches a unit on death and dying, and she uses it to impress upon her students her reasons for insisting on excellence from them. Each fall she tells her students five things that are important to her. One of them is that she had a child who died. She tells her pupils, "She doesn't have the opportunity to make the most of her life, but you do. You're alive. You're here. I feel like you have some purpose, and if I see you're not trying to take advantage of it, I'm going to be impatient." Her students respond well to her transparency. "They're always receptive of that."

Twyla, whose second child was stillborn, made plans to incorporate her experience into her new photography business after learning about professional photographers who come in and take pictures of stillborn babies for the parents. "I think that's something I might do. Because they don't have anything. You need to acknowledge that there was a loss."

Lyn and Sherri aren't the same people they were before they lost their daughter. They've changed, and so have Jeff, Carolyn, and Twyla, along with every parent who has lost a child. It took a long, long time for each one to pick through the brokenness littering their worlds. But along the way, they grew into strong, compassionate, grateful people.

One day, you, too, will make your way through the devastation that shattered your world. Your world will be changed. And you'll be changed, too.

Father, the death of my child shattered my world. I'm not the same person I once was. Help me find my way through the effects of this loss and find a purpose to live again. Show me how to live as a changed person.

How did becoming a parent change your world? How did your child's illness shake your world? What shattered in your world when your child died?

Take Time to Reflect

50

Remember the Child

> "Oh! Ephraim is my dear, dear son,
>   my child in whom I take pleasure!
> Every time I mention his name,
>   my heart bursts with longing for him!
> Everything in me cries out for him.
> Softly and tenderly I wait for him."
>
> Jeremiah 31:20

When the loss of your child is recent, your memories are vivid and painful. Each vision of the little face, each whiff of the unique scent of sweat and dirt and baby shampoo, each repetition of a pet phrase or taste of a favorite treat rips your heart. Every memory creates a sharp longing within you. You wonder if you will ever be able to think of your child with joy instead of sorrow, with laughter instead of tears.

Sandy, whose son Ethan died at birth, says she waited a long time for her memories to bring joy instead of sorrow. For the first few years the anniversary of her son's birth and death, August 7, was not a good day. But about five years after he died, a friend sent two roses to Sandy while she was at work. Sandy asked why she'd sent the flowers. "Isn't tomorrow Ethan's birthday?" the friend asked.

That's when it hit Sandy. "I have finally gotten over the top of the mountain, and I'm on the downhill side," she thought. "It's not affecting me the same way it had before. The devastation—I got past the devastation and went on to whatever God was going to do with it."

You hope to move past the devastation, also. But at the same time, you want to keep your memories from fading away. Sandy keeps that from happening by thumbing through Ethan's album now and then. She looks at his pictures, the cards people sent, his little preemie outfit and the blanket he was wrapped in, his tiny hospital wristband. She can now do this without being overwhelmed by despair. "It reminds me of what wouldn't have happened if he hadn't been born." She now views Ethan's short life as a positive instead of a negative. "But it took a long time to get there."

Sherri, who lost her daughter in 1964, says she often thinks about Sherri Lyn on her birthday. Whenever she and her husband, Lyn, go to the town where their infant daughter is buried, they drive through the cemetery. "You think about all the things that happened," Lyn says "That's part of you. You don't forget that."

If Carolyn's daughter Beth were alive, she would be a young woman now. Even though decades have passed since her death, Carolyn says sometimes it seems like it all happened just yesterday. The milestone moments, like weddings and graduations of people Beth's age, trigger her memories and keep them fresh.

Memories, so sharp and clear you will think it happened yesterday, will come to you. Your tears will surprise you, but your emotions are normal. Even Brenda, whose son Jeff is living but mentally and physically disabled, experiences similar cycles of grief. "Birthdays and certain celebrations will trigger those old emotions," she says. "You think you've dealt with them. You have dealt with them, but they come back."

But take heart. One day you will climb past the devastation and reach the top of your mountain. There, you will linger over memories of your child's life and rejoice to see the good that happened because your child was born. You will examine the person you've become, the person you could not have been without the life and death of your child. You will think of how God worked in your child's short life, how He used everything to shape your compassion and strength. And you will be glad because that part of you deep inside is anchored so hard and fast that you will always, always remember your child with joy.

Dear Father, I want to remember my child, but it hurts. My memories bring both joy and pain. Each day, give me what I need to cope. Help me climb my mountain of devastation so one day I can come down the other side.

When do the memories of your child bring you comfort? When do they bring you pain? How do you cope with the devastation some memories bring?

Take Time to Reflect

A Different Dream Begins

Raising a Survivor

51

Survivor: Kids' Edition

He has blocked my ways with hewn stone;
He has made my paths crooked.

From Jeremiah's complaint
about God in Lamentations 3:9 (NASB)

When first I heard about the TV show *Survivor*, I told my family, "We aren't going to watch it. Who needs fake obstacles when life is full of real ones?"

I wasn't thinking only of the obstacles our family had overcome when I announced the ban. I was thinking of some of my former elementary students and the obstacles they'd faced in their young lives. They hadn't retrieved forty-pound rocks from the ocean floor or hiked eleven miles through the jungle. They hadn't dragged a 250-pound dummy across an obstacle course. They didn't need to, because they knew plenty about obstacles. They were already survivors.

Nic was one of those students. When he walked into my classroom, he looked like an ordinary fourth grader. Some time later, his parents told me Nic had survived cancer. He'd been diagnosed with Stage IV neuroblastoma when he was three. After months of aggressive chemo, radiation, surgery, and a bone marrow transplant, he'd gone into remission.

Nic's fourth grade year was ordinary. He was a good student, a hard worker, popular with classmates, and he always had a smile on his face. The smile turned into a grin when he told me his annual cancer check had been clear.

But three years later, the cancer reappeared in his left thigh bone. He spent the spring of his seventh grade year and most of his eighth grade year undergoing treatment until the disease went into remission again.

I tracked Nic's progress at his CaringBridge Web site. The summer after he finished eighth grade, when he was fourteen, I visited him and his family. Sitting at his kitchen table, I asked him how surviving cancer had changed his outlook on life.

"Well, anything can be thrown at you, pretty much." Then Nic described a worksheet he'd been given in school. It was titled "Your Goal" and had a place to write a goal. Then, there were roadblocks where each student wrote what had happened in his life. "So it kind of showed you what you go through to get your goal. So you could see it's not always a straight path. You have to get stuff. You have to go through stuff."

"Do you think you understood that paper better than your classmates?" I asked.

"Kinda, yeah … 'cause, like cancer, it slows you down. You have to go through all the stuff for it."

"And what did you appreciate most about your parents when you faced those obstacles?"

"That they were there for me," Nic answered.

You were at the obstacle course, too, watching your child fight for life. It was hard. You wanted to push away the barriers. You hated to see your child face so many road-blocks at such a young age. You watched and cheered as your child overcame them. And when your child became a survivor, you were right there, where you'd been all along.

As I drove home, Nic's words echoed in my thoughts:

"… anything can be thrown at you …"

"… it's not always a straight path."

"… cancer, it slows you down. You have to go through all the stuff for it."

Dragging a 250-pound dummy through an obstacle course is child's play compared to what Nic has gone through. A million-dollar prize is nothing compared to the persever-ance he's shown. Watching strangers conquer fake challenges on TV is nothing compared to talking to a fourteen-year-old whose parents stood on the sidelines and cheered him on while he fought for his life and won.

Who needs fake survivors when the world is full of real ones?

Father, thank you for granting my child restored health. Thank you for the privilege of cheering from the sidelines throughout this long ordeal. Thank you for these obstacles that have made us into a family of survivors.

What were the greatest obstacles your child overcame during illness? How did those obstacles strengthen you and your child?

Take Time to Reflect

52

A Treasure of Goodness

> Summing it all up, friends, I'd say you'll do best by filling your minds and meditating on things true, noble, reputable, authentic, compelling, gracious—the best, not the worst; the beautiful, not the ugly; things to praise, not things to curse.
>
> Philippians 4:8

Nic's parents, Travis and Jamie, are survivors, too. Since their son's cancer reoccurred and went into remission again, Jamie says she's become paranoid. When Grace, their toddler, is fussy, she wonders if her daughter has cancer. The same thought crosses her mind if Nic mentions something as small as a headache.

You know all about those thought patterns, because you share them. When illness pierced the illusion of your ability to control the bad things in your child's life, you became paranoid, too. I sure did. Every time the doctors explained a new complication, a new paranoia materialized, and I proceeded to worry over it vigilantly. Who knew the esophagus was so dangerous?

But Travis and Jamie said Nic's illness and survival also led to positive changes in their parenting. "Look at our house," Jamie says. "Normally there's clean laundry piled on that chair. But it sits there because Nic says, 'Let's go on a walk,' or 'Let's go on a bike ride,' or 'Let's go to the pool.' And that's so much more important, and it's more fun, too."

I wish I'd been more like Jamie, more willing to play and less concerned about housework, when my kids were young. But I responded in different ways. Creating and preserving family memories became my passion. We attended more family reunions and visited relatives more often. I took scads of pictures and wrote childhood stories to pass on to our kids and grandkids some day.

Hiram took Allen and Anne on long hikes by the river and on adventures in the nearby state park. At bedtime, he told them stories about his childhood in Alaska, stories they still laugh about even though they're now adults.

Travis cherishes spending time with Nic and describes a recent four-wheeler trip they took. "We drove up to my dad's farm. We spent as much time driving as we did playing, probably more by the time we hooked up the trailer and unloaded." Travis could have decided the trip was a waste of time. But he didn't. "It was worth it," he explains, "because I know I'll remember that day for a long time, and I hope that Nic does, too."

Your child's illness is burned into your memory. You can't and shouldn't try to erase those memories, because they're part of who you are. But you can and should balance those memories with new, happier ones now that your child is healthy.

That's why Travis goes four-wheeling with Nic. "All those memories we make—those are something for us to fall back on in hard times. Because you realize the good times you have, when you have the bad times."

Someday your family will experience another hard time, maybe in the form of illness or a tragic accident, or a grandparent will die of old age, or you may lose your job. In those hard times, remember how Christ led your family through suffering to survival and made you stronger when your child was ill. Open the treasure chest of memories you've created since then: trips to the pool, walks by the river, visits with relatives, bedtime stories, and four-wheeling at the farm.

Fill your minds with good memories until you and your children see the source of every good gift—the best, the beautiful, the One to praise—God the Father, who revealed himself to us in Jesus Christ His Son.

God who is with us, you were present when our child was sick, and you are present now. We trust you to be present in the good and bad times to come. During the good times, teach us to store up memories that will carry us through whatever lies ahead.

What are some of your favorite family memories? What good, new memories do you want to create with your kids? How will you begin?

Take Time to Reflect

The Place Where I Grew Up

> "All the others gave what they'll never miss; she gave extravagantly what she couldn't afford—she gave her all."
>
> Mark 12:44

When I graduated from high school, I claimed my hometown as the place where I grew up. After I received my undergraduate degree, I decided I'd grown up at college. Once my husband and I accumulated a few years of job experience, I was sure we were both adults. When Allen was born and the adventure of hospital parenting made me feel old and tired, I was convinced I'd grown up.

233

I discovered I was wrong one November day, six months after our son's birth. A few weeks earlier, friends in our tiny South Dakota town held a fundraiser to help defray Allen's mounting medical expenses. Although it was 1982 and Camp Crook's population was less than 100 people, over $1,500 was raised.

Almost everyone in town attended, along with people from all over the county and from across the Montana and North Dakota state lines. The only townspeople not in attendance were our nearest neighbors, Walter and Pearl. Dirt poor, they lived in a little tar paper shack with a hoard of cats. A scrap lumber fence surrounded their garden. Scarecrows made of old work shirts and cowboy hats watched over the neat rows of vegetables that provided most of their food.

Every week Walter pushed his wheelbarrow to the dump. "Yes sir, Philo," he told my husband. "Yes sir, I got me a deal with the city to clean up the dump. Yep, I go out there and keep it neat for the city, I do. Yep, I load up stuff just layin' around, old wood and the like, and take it off their hands for 'em. Yep, old Walter's a worker. You just ask anybody."

Walter and Pearl's acquaintance with Allen was limited to visits at the church potlucks they attended religiously. Pearl always placed a quart of her canned pickled beets on the serving table, but no one ever ate them since cat hairs floated in the ruby-colored brine.

One Sunday after Pearl cleaned her plate and went back for second helpings, she wandered over to Allen and me. She patted his head, and the crease between her eyes deepened as I poured milk down his feeding tube. "He gonna be all right?"

"After a few more surgeries he'll be fine," I assured her.

She chucked him under the chin. "Awful expensive, ain't it?"

I nodded.

Since a potluck meal wasn't part of Allen's fundraiser, I wasn't surprised by Walter and Pearl's absence at the gala event. Anyway, I told myself, they have nothing to give.

A few weeks later, I pulled a lumpy, dirty envelope from our post office box. A collection of stamps nearly covered the front of it. The succinct address scrawled below the stamps—Philo Camp Crook—was barely legible.

I opened the envelope and shook a brightly colored plastic teething ring into my hand, along with a grimy piece of paper. I unfolded the paper, removed three worn dollar bills from inside it, then read the short note. "For the boy," it said. "Love, Walter and Pearl."

I stood in the post office and blinked away tears. Right there, right then, in the presence of Christ's sacrificial love made real in my life, I grew up.

Walter and Pearl, along with many other people, became Christ to us during Allen's illness. Their examples showed us how to grow in our love toward others. They gave extravagantly beyond what they had, they cared for the weak and the hurting, they considered others more important than themselves.

You'll grow, too, as Christ enters your circumstances. He'll reveal himself through people you tend to discount, in the places you least expect. Wherever you are when you comprehend the extent of His sacrificial love at work in your life, that's the place where you will finally and completely grow up.

Dear Father, I am humbled by the extravagant sacrifices people have made on our child's behalf. Thank you for using them to help us survive this difficult time. Thank you for revealing yourself to me and helping me grow up.

Who has given to you beyond what they had to give? How have you seen Christ in their generosity? How have you grown through these experiences?

Take Time to Reflect

54

Let Them Be Kids; Teach Them to Be Adults

> Also, guide the young men to live disciplined lives. But mostly, show them all this by doing it yourself.
>
> Titus 2:6–7

Every time Allen was in the hospital I wanted the doctors to fix the latest complication so our son could be a typical kid. My desire may have been a little unrealistic, but for the most part it was fulfilled. The doctors fixed most of his problems, and Allen's pronouncement concerning his childhood is, "I was a normal kid."

But his illness affected the way my husband and I parented our son. After four years of surgeries, procedures, intermittent crises, and prolonged sleep deprivation, we didn't know how to act once Allen's esophagus functioned properly. For us, the transition from parenting a sick kid to raising a healthy one was bumpy. We had to let him explore the world without weighing him down with memories of his illness, and teach him to live a full life without becoming reckless and exacerbating his condition.

Twyla walked the same tightrope as she raised her son Austin, who has severe asthma. "You have to let them be kids," she says. "You can't hold them back from trying things because they have this condition." But, she states, as kids get older they also must learn to become responsible for their own care.

If your child is quite young, you think there's plenty of time to address self-care issues. In truth, you should start long before adolescence begins. Many kids who are sick as youngsters go into denial during their teen years. They want to be like their friends. They want to eat what everyone else does, play the same games and sports, participate in the same clubs and activities. For teen boys, the pressure to conform to tough physical standards is especially powerful. Young male culture revolves around being big, strong, and fast. To fit into that culture, young men will ignore medical restrictions related to a former or a chronic condition.

You need to equip your young child now. Since example is the best teacher, make sure your lifestyle is a balanced mix of healthy activity, proactive health care, and respect for wise counsel from doctors for your child to imitate. Explain your health choices to your child and relate them to the choices they have to make. Educate your child early about managing health restrictions concerning diet, activity, medications, and rest. The sooner they take ownership of the restrictions, the less likely they are to abandon them when they are older.

As children who once had serious health conditions mature, they need to know the part their conditions play in adult life. They should be able to summarize their health history for doctors. They should know how a pre-existing health condition affects their ability to obtain insurance, whether genetic counseling is needed before they conceive children, and the ramifications their health condition has on pregnancy and childbirth. These special considerations, added to the mountain of responsibilities that accompany entry into adulthood, are enough to push a young adult into denial again. Your job as a parent is to encourage your child to be responsible about personal health and to provide a safe place to ask for advice when it's needed.

It's not an easy job, and Hiram and I didn't do it perfectly. We couldn't have done it at all without our faith in God's presence. We prayed often, tried to be good examples, and waited … and waited … for our labors to bear fruit.

One day, when Allen was in his early twenties, he called with a surprising announcement. "I've scheduled a scope of my upper G.I. You guys said I should have one every two years. It's about time I got on the ball about it."

When he spoke, a weight lifted from my shoulders. "He's done it," I told my husband after I hung up the phone. "Allen's become an adult."

Dear Father, I thought parenting would be easier once my child was well again. But I need your guidance to parent a healthy kid wisely. Teach me the proper balance between letting my child be normal and demonstrating how to be responsible for a health condition.

When is it hard for you to let your child be a normal, healthy kid? What health care responsibilities do you need to teach your child? When will you start and what is your plan?

Take Time to Reflect

55

From Victim to Survivor

God makes everything come out right;
He puts victims back on their feet.

Psalm 103:6

The shoe salesman slid Allen's small feet into new snow
boots, then stood him on the floor to check their fit. Allen,
three or four at the time, sighed his gurgly sigh. The man
looked up, surprised by the sound. Our little boy put on his
best victim face and explained, "I have a problem with my
esophagus."

The salesman was instantly solicitous and treated Allen
like royalty. Our son left the store wearing his new boots. I
left the store worried by our pint-sized manipulator's ability
to use his condition to solicit attention and special treatment.
His newly acquired victim mentality needed to be eliminated

quickly or he wouldn't know how to function in the healthy world he would soon enter.

Angie, Chandler's mom, worried about her nine-year-old son as he neared the end of three and a half years of treatment for his leukemia. Her concerns weren't so much about a reoccurrence of cancer, since his had gone into remission shortly after treatment began, and his prognosis was excellent. Instead, she was worried about the attitude he'd developed. "He's still very manipulative. As soon as he's in the hospital for a spinal tap, which only takes an hour, he becomes the victim, even though he's perfectly healthy," Angie says. "He doesn't want to get out of bed. He doesn't want to grab his own water."

"Emotionally," she adds, "he still struggles. With some things he's very mature, and in other ways he's very far behind." One of her greatest desires is for Chandler to develop a new attitude when his treatment ends, so he'll fit into society and be a productive person, not a victim.

Parents can develop a victim mentality, too. I know because it happened to me. The crisis atmosphere created by Allen's illness was seductive. People jumped in to relieve me of the ordinary, everyday pressures of life. They treated me differently, and I got used to the nice things done on my behalf, the special breaks I received.

When each crisis passed and I returned to normal life and the mundane issues that populate it—paying the bills, mowing the lawn, going to work—I had a hard time being part of the crowd again. Sometimes I longed for a new health crisis and the balloon bouquets, cards, and sympathy bound to accompany it.

When I observed my son playing the role of victim to perfection, I knew he was copying me. My mentality needed to transform from victim to survivor so Allen could imitate a healthy example. But I couldn't accomplish the transformation on my own, so I asked God to step in and change first me, then our son.

In our case, God used circumstances to put my feet on solid ground again. New jobs took our family to a town where no one knew about Allen's early struggles. As a result, no one treated him as a sick kid, and before long, I didn't either. In fact, I soon insisted he do as much as possible for himself and encouraged him to try new things. Although it took time, his victim mentality and mine faded, and we dealt with ordinary life like ordinary people.

If you detect a victim mentality in yourself or in your child, ask God, and He will transform your thinking and behavior. Ask Him to empower you to cope with the pressures of everyday life. Ask Him to show you how to treat your child normally. Ask Him to give your child the mindset and behaviors of a healthy kid. Ask Him to do whatever it takes to prepare your child for life in normal society as a productive citizen.

God answered my prayer by moving us to a new town. And you can trust Him to answer your earnest parent's prayer, too. He wants your child to be a survivor, not a victim.

Dear Father, give me eyes to detect any signs of victim mentality in our family. Give me wisdom to lay those attitudes before you so you can change them. Teach us to live as a normal, healthy family.

When is it easy for your child to shift into a victim mentality? When is it easy for you? What steps do you need to take to change the way you and your child think?

Take Time to Reflect

56

We Rejoiced to Hear Him Cry

My eyes are blind with tears, my stomach in a knot.
My insides have turned to jelly over my people's
fate.
Babies and children are fainting all over the place,
Calling to their mothers, "I'm hungry! I'm thirsty!"
Lamentations 2:11–12

Parents take the blessings of life with a healthy child for granted. While a child is very ill, the priceless value of good health comes into sharp focus. But when life regains a semblance of normalcy, appreciation for God's daily blessings often fades away.

Dave and Christy regained their appreciation for those blessings soon after their son AJ was diagnosed with Crohn's disease. AJ wasn't responding to treatment, and the new doctor on the case ordered another colonoscopy for the little boy. Because of a hospital remodeling project, the colonoscopy had to be performed in the Pediatric Intensive Care Unit (PICU).

Dave and Christy walked up to the PICU and passed a room packed with people, so full that many spilled into the hallway. But Dave's thoughts were focused on his son, so he didn't pay much attention when they walked by the crowded room. "AJ's got to go through this again," he worried. "He's not feeling well. His Crohn's is flaring up again. He's got to have another colonoscopy."

The parents' waiting area was close to the room where the colonoscopy was performed. AJ was partially sedated, and though he didn't know what was going on, he talked and whimpered during the procedure. Dave and Christy heard him cry out, "Mommy, Mommy!" several times.

"It was a horrible feeling for us," Dave says. "So unsettling." To get away from the sound, they walked down the hall. As they went by the crowded hospital room they had barely noticed earlier, they saw nurses crying as they left it. "There was a child dying in there," Dave says. "This was the last hour of this child's life. I tell you, it hit us hard."

Christy nods. "We realized those parents would have given anything to hear their child cry."

Subdued, they returned to the waiting area. They thought of the parents in the other room, watching the life ebb from their child's body. Suddenly the inconveniences that blocked their appreciation of the daily blessings in their lives—AJ's frequent tummy aches, inconvenient doctor visits, and his regime of medicines—faded away. They listened to their son's plaintive weeping with a new outlook. "We knew that if those parents in the other room could trade places with us, they would," Dave says. "And we rejoiced to hear our boy cry."

If life is settling into a comfortable routine now that your child's health has improved, your appreciation of God's daily blessings in your life may begin to fade away. You'll be tempted to overlook the priceless value of your child's good health.

As everyday life presses down, you'll be tempted to grumble about how much the grocery bill has gone up now that your child has an appetite again. You'll be tempted to complain about how your kid outgrew an expensive, new dress shirt in a month, and tore a pair of blue jeans during a flag football game. You'll be tempted to grouse about the cost and inconvenience of the annual well-child visit at the doctor's office. And you'll be tempted to walk away and feel sorry for yourself when your child is irrationally upset about some stupid little thing and won't stop crying, "Mommy! Daddy!"

When those temptations arise, close your eyes. Picture your child in the hospital, fighting for life. Think about the children down the hall who didn't survive, and the grieving parents who lost them. Count your child's sobs and whimpers as blessings. Rejoice when your child cries.

Dear Father, my child's illness showed me the value of life and health. Forgive me for overlooking today's daily blessings. Teach me to appreciate all of life, including the cries of my child.

How did your child's illness and recovery make you more aware of daily blessings? When are you tempted to take them for granted? How can you keep that from happening?

Take Time to Reflect

Each Day Is a Gift

Children who defeat a serious illness often return to healthy life without grasping how close they came to death. In the hospital they were too sick to understand the gravity of the situation. And once they've recovered and are active again, they're still too young to comprehend what happened. For them, ignorance is bliss.

But as parents of a child who survived a brush with death, bliss comes not from ignorance, but from the new lease on life the child has received. Parents watch their carefree, healthy kids and wonder if they will ever be fully grateful for this second chance at life.

I was never sure how to approach the topic as Allen grew up. Most of his treatment occurred before he was five, so he has only fragmented memories of it. We didn't want to dwell on his early illness, but we did want him to know what others had done to save his life. So as he grew we told him stories of the doctors and his hospital stays. We emphasized the kindnesses shown to us by others and our gratitude for God's hand over our family.

Finally, when Allen was in his early twenties and his friends started to have children, his early history made an impression on him. "Mom, they're the same age you were when I was born," he said during a phone call. "You were awfully young when you went through all that." As he compared those children and his early years, he became more serious about life, more purposeful in his choices, more grateful.

The gift of renewed health changed Jenny, too. She was older during her fight against acute lymphocytic leukemia (ALL) and remembers much of it. "It made me grow up really fast," she says. "I don't know if it's the whole maturing process or if it's what goes along with all that treatment," she adds. "Maybe that's an adjustment that comes with losing that childhood innocence."

She says her priorities have always been different than those of her peers. "The things that were important to them just weren't to me, even in college." She believes her illness had a great deal to do with who she is. "I'm more oriented toward a relationship, like a stronger relationship with God. I feel there's a reason I'm still here. That has a lot to do with my outlook on life. I've got something I need to do while I'm here. I have a bigger picture sense of things than I might have had, like a draw toward helping people. That has a lot to do with what happened, because I had ALL."

If you wonder whether your child will value this second chance at life, or ever be grateful for the pain endured, let Jenny's story bring you hope. She endured countless blood draws, weeks in hospital isolation, numerous cycles of chemotherapy, hair loss, and a compromised immune system that resulted in two years of home schooling and a month quarantined from her siblings when they had chicken pox. Still, she is grateful for the experience and the person she is because of it.

Someday, most likely on the heels of adulthood, your child will also express gratitude for the gift of renewed life. Until then, you have to wait patiently and be grateful in your son's or daughter's stead. While you wait, ask God to give your child the capacity to echo Jenny's words, born of gratitude for her second chance to live: "Try to appreciate all that you have, like your health. It's a gift. Each day is a blessing."

Dear Father, thank you for granting my child a second chance at life. Make me a grateful parent and shape my child into a grateful adult, purposefully using the gift of life in a way that pleases you.

How has your child's life blessed you today? How can you express gratitude for that blessing?

Take Time to Reflect

58

Rub My Cheek

People brought babies to Jesus, hoping he
might touch them.

Luke 18:15

During Allen's first hospitalization, a nurse offered some advice we used long after we knew our son would survive. "Babies need touch," the nurse said. "I hold Allen as much as possible, but I have other infants assigned to me, too. The more you can be here and hold him, the faster he'll recover. Do exactly what you would do if you were home together. Look at him, talk to him, and touch him, even when he has to be in the incubator."

Hiram made the nurse's directive his mission and spent every available moment with our son, holding him as much as they let him. I was still recovering from pregnancy and childbirth and using the breast pump four times a day; I was exhausted after a morning in NICU. After lunch, Hiram took me to our room for a nap. Then he went back to the hospital. "When he needs to be in the incubator, I put my hands through the openings on the side and rub his cheek," Hiram explained one day when he returned from his vigil.

One morning a nurse pulled me aside. "We've never seen anything like this. Your husband sits on a stool beside Allen's Isolette for hours. He's a very special daddy."

"It may have something to do with his work with delinquent teenage boys," I told her. "He's seen so many sons abandoned by their fathers. He wants Allen to know his dad loves him and won't leave him."

Throughout Allen's NICU stay, Hiram sat beside the Isolette hour after hour, day after day, rubbing his son's tiny cheek. Once Allen came home, as we nursed him through numerous complications, Hiram often spent the night in the recliner rocker holding Allen and rubbing his cheek, until they both fell into a fitful, upright sleep.

In spite of everything, Allen thrived. He reached physical milestones after most children and was small for his age, but he was alert and responsive to people. He was curious and outgoing. Even so, until he was ten or twelve, whenever he was upset or scared, sick or in pain, he ran to his father. Safe in Hiram's arms, he begged, "Dad, rub my cheek," and lifted his face to his father's loving hand.

Hiram's constant, faithful touch had a powerful effect on Allen for years after his illness. Your gentle touch can have the same effect on your child. When your child was sick, you offered your healing touch automatically when you rocked together, patted a diapered bottom, held a small hand. Now that your child is healthy, keep doing the same thing.

God created us to be healed by His loving touch. All it took for Jesus to heal the blind, the lame, the deaf, the dumb, and the lepers was the touch of His hand. Mothers brought their babies, sick or healthy, hoping Jesus would touch and strengthen them. They knew God's powerful touch brings wholeness to His children.

Your touch is God's healing hand upon your child's body. Your gentle caress is as necessary to your child's health as food and water, shelter and clothing, light and air. Your hand upon a tiny cheek will begin to heal the inward scars of illness: the pain of surgery, the fear of separation, the despair of illness. It will help your child thrive in spite of illness and promote continued wholeness even after a complete recovery.

Your healthy child needs your healing touch. So as often as you can, ruffle that head of wispy hair. Kiss a soft forehead. Massage a little back. Rub a tiny cheek. Bring your baby to Jesus. With your hand, show your child His constant touch.

Father, thank you for creating us to be healed by your touch. Thank you for allowing me to be your hand of healing in my child's life. Show me how to reach out to my child in ways that honor you.

What kind of touch soothes your child? How can you express your love for your child through touch?

Take Time to Reflect

59

Complete the Healing

"He won't brush aside the bruised and the hurt
and he won't disregard the small and
insignificant,
but he'll steadily and firmly set things right."

Isaiah 42:3

After Allen's first surgery and throughout his child-hood, whenever we consulted with doctors and surgeons, we asked the same questions: "Will the trauma and pain he experienced affect him emotionally? Is there anything we should be doing to help him?"

The doctors would visit and play with our curious, talkative, confident son and downplay our concerns, say-ing, "He's obviously a happy child. Chances are he doesn't remember any of it, so keep doing what you're doing."

At first we agreed with the doctors; but as Allen grew older, he developed a disturbing behavior pattern. Whenever our normally conscientious, people-pleasing son felt trapped, he either shut down and refused to discuss the situation or responded in irrational, destructive ways. We suspected deep emotional wounds festered even though his physical scars had faded away. He was in college before we found professionals who confirmed our suspicion: There was a link between the medical trauma he had suffered and his behavior. Allen was a young adult before he confronted the destructive habits he'd developed and sought help to change them.

The doctors were not to blame for their advice. A generation earlier, they wouldn't have had the medical knowledge to save Allen's life. By the time he was born, they could heal his body, but not his emotions. It took another generation before the medical community knew how to heal both. In fact, the organization that developed the treatments, the Child Life Council, wasn't created until the year Allen was born, 1982.

If your child was treated recently at a major medical center or children's hospital, a Child Life specialist probably met with you and worked with your child, alleviating trauma through role play that showed what happens during surgery and treatment. And they educated you about how to remain calm and provide support.

But if your child was treated at a small hospital or in an emergency room, the assistance might not have been available. In that case, it's up to you to address the effects of medical trauma, even before you see evidence of it. Otherwise emotional wounds may fester below the surface, and the habits your child develops to cope with them could become ingrained, destructive behaviors.

God doesn't want your child to go through life emotionally bruised and hurt, suffering from post-traumatic stress disorder (PTSD). He wants to heal even the smallest, most insignificant wound hiding within your child's heart. As surely as He provided doctors to heal your child's body, He can provide counselors and therapists to heal the effects of trauma, too.

If you suspect your child is suffering from PTSD, do whatever it takes to find help. If your hospital doesn't have a Child Life specialist, contact large medical centers, university hospitals, or children's hospitals in your area until you reach one. Explain the situation and seek advice and information on the topic. Ask if someone at the hospital can meet with your child or if they can recommend therapists. Don't stop until you find someone who can help.

I couldn't change my son's past. But I could and did stand by him when he sought treatment for PTSD as a young adult. And I can urge you to take advantage of treatments not available when he was a child. If our experience can help your family, my husband and son and I will be thankful. The opportunity to help your child heals us, too. It's evidence of God at work, using our story in some way to help steadily and firmly set all things right.

Father of all healing, thank you for the doctors who healed our child's body. Thank you for Child Life specialists and counselors who can heal emotions, too. Lead us to godly, loving therapists who can provide the help we need.

What evidence do you see of emotional healing in your child? What concerns do you have about your child's emotional healing? Who can help you address those concerns?

Take Time to Reflect

60

I Know Good Came from It

We continue to shout our praise even when
we're hemmed in with troubles, because we
know how troubles can develop passionate
patience in us, and how that patience in turn
forges the tempered steel of virtue, keeping us
alert for whatever God will do next.

Romans 5:3–4

Sue was two and a half when she decided to do the
laundry. While her mom was outside hanging clothes on
the line, she pushed a stool against the electric wringer
washing machine and tried to feed the clothes through the
rollers with her hands. Her mother found her with both
arms caught in the roller, the machine still running, the skin

peeled from her arms, exposing bone and muscle. The scars remain to this day.

A few years later, doctors discovered that the accident had damaged the growth plate in one arm. The bone that lengthens the arm was growing sideways. To repair the damage Sue went through six surgeries, starting in kindergarten and ending after her junior year in high school.

Sue doesn't remember the accident, and her memories of the early surgeries are sketchy. What she does remember is the resilience of the kids she met in the hospital throughout the years. "You go to an adult ward and everyone is moaning and groaning. But the kids are amazing," she says. "They don't know they're hurt. They don't know they're sick. They're happy no matter what."

Her experiences also changed her relationships with children outside the hospital. One of her classmates was ostracized by the other students. "Michelle didn't come from a good home," says Sue. "She was never clean, she never looked nice. The teachers always put me with her." Later, after the girl moved away, Sue's mom told her the reason the teachers always paired her with Michelle was "because I was more compassionate with her. I would actually play with her. I was her only friend."

Sue's injuries weren't life threatening, but her scars made her self-conscious. "Scars aren't a pleasant thing. I would position my arms so you couldn't see the scars. And long sleeves were a good thing." She finally got over her self-consciousness when a boy asked her out. "If the boys don't care," she thought, "why should I care?"

That confidence booster combined with an encounter during her final hospital stay significantly altered her perspective of life. "When I was a junior, for some reason they put me on the pediatric ward." In the game room, she and a little boy with a brain tumor became pals. His surgery was very risky, and he didn't survive. Sue remembers thinking, "Here I'm moping about having this arm injury, even after the doctor said it was amazing it didn't damage the functioning of my hand. And this poor boy goes in for brain surgery and he never came back out again." She adds, "That was a reality check for me."

Now a wife and mom of two boys, Sue looks back on her childhood without minimizing her struggles. "I missed out on a lot. Usually I had surgeries in the summer, six of them in a twelve-year period. So in every summer picture, I have a cast on. I missed out on so much, the fun things like swimming. So I kind of resented it growing up." She pauses to think. "But I know good came from it. Even then, I think I knew that, too."

Parents want to protect their children. They often try to minimize the pain experienced and the normal childhood activities stolen by illness. But God never asks you to diminish your struggles or your child's. Instead, He calls us to acknowledge them and to trust Him to turn loss and pain into the tempered steel of virtue within us and our children. Once His work is complete, you will look back together and say, "We know good came from it."

Dear Father, you gave life to my child, and I am grateful. But I worry about what my child lost to illness. Help us find good in what happened, and help us to trust you while you complete your work in all of us.

What did illness steal from your child? How did illness strengthen your child and you? What good has come from it already?

Take Time to Reflect

Living a Different Dream

Don't you wish life fit into convenient segments like the devotions in this book? Wouldn't it be wonderful if your child's condition was resolved and the need for treatment ended when you reached the last page? But we both know that life, especially with a chronically or critically ill child, is rarely convenient. No matter how graciously you have accepted your child's prognosis or how well you've adjusted to the demands of this new dream, difficulties may continue for many weeks, months, or even years.

When we were in the middle of caring for our very ill son, I longed to talk to moms and dads who had experienced what our family was living. But caring for Allen was all-consuming, and I didn't have time or energy to locate anyone. After his health condition moderated and our lives resumed a more normal pattern, my desire to connect with families going through similar circumstances continued. I wanted someone to develop a community that brought parents together and linked them to people and resources able to provide assistance and encouragement. Slowly, patiently God put me in a place where I could accomplish for other families what I wanted for my own.

The publication of this book provided the opportunity to begin an online community on the Web at The Different Dream Web site(www.differentdream.com). The site is designed to educate parents about medical conditions and the effects of medical trauma on children. It also addresses spiritual concerns parents have for their children and provides a supportive, encouraging online community where parents can seek advice and share the challenges they face as parents of sick kids.

At the Web site you can order resources and find links related to specific childhood diseases and health conditions. While you're there, send me an e-mail or leave a comment at the blog about the dreams you have for your child.

Note to the Reader

The publisher invites you to share your response to the message of this book by writing:

> Discovery House Publishers
> P.O. Box 3566
> Grand Rapids, MI 49501
> U.S.A.

For information about other Discovery House books, music, videos, or DVDs, contact us at the same address or call 1-800-653-8333. Find us on the Internet at http://www.dhp.org/ or send e-mail to books@dph.org.